the girls' guide to
SURVIVING A
BREAKUP

the girls' guide to
SURVIVING A
BREAKUP

DELPHINE HIRSH

ST. MARTIN'S GRIFFIN

NEW YORK

www.stmartins.com

illustrations by Chris Long/CWC International, Inc.

Library of Congress Cataloging-in-Publication Data

Hirsh, Delphine.
    The girls' guide to surviving a breakup / Delphine Hirsh.
        p. cm.
    ISBN 0-312-28519-1
        1. Man-woman relationships. 2. Separation (Psychology)—
Popular works. 3. Adjustment (Psychology)—Popular works. 4.
Women—Psychology. I. Title.
HQ801.A3 H57 2003
306.7—dc21   2002028135

10 9 8 7 6

FOR
my mother Sabine
Leora
Eliza
Heather W.
Sharon
Lisa
Valerie
Heather M.
Diane
Dara
Gwen
Eva

AND IN MEMORY
my grandmother Ruth
Priscilla
Nancy

Contents

Acknowledgments

I would like to thank the many people who helped with this book in one way or another: my colleagues from amfAR, Dave Bear, Barbara Berkowitz, the Burkleys, the Chestons, Maria Gabriela Cowperwaithe, Heather Cochran, Dennis Dennehy, Ed Eglin, Jake and Hilary Elkins, the Farbers, Jamie Fenwick, Stephanie Furman, Virginia Gilbert, the Goldbergers, Nick Gomez, Mariana Gosnell, Jane and Jim Hutchins, Julia Kalantarova, Tim Kernan, Michelle Labranche, Kendall LaMontagne, Chris Long, Gretchen Long, Mary Marcus, Tim Mendelson, Liz McNamara, Pamela and Gifford Miller, Robert Morris, Marjorie Schwartz Nielsen, Deneen and Colin O'Neill, Jeff Polacheck, Kwami Reynolds, Chris Riley and the Rileys, the Robinsons, Scott Skey, Susan Solomon, and Ruth Solomon. I would like to thank the fabulous Charlene English for helping me get the word out. I am very grateful for the contributions of the incredible team at St. Martin's and, in particular, thank: Kim Cardascia, Wah-Ming Chang, Cynthia Merman, Marshall Presnick, and Jennifer Reeve. I am especially grateful to my dynamite editor, Jennifer Enderlin, for her enthusiasm and invaluable work. I am also lucky to have the best, most brilliant agent, Theresa Park, who made this project happen, and to also have had the assistance of her charming associate, Julie Barer. And last, but never least, I am fortunate to have the three greatest and most supportive men in my life: my father, M. A. Farber; my brother, Christophe Farber; and my husband, Adam Hirsh.

Introduction

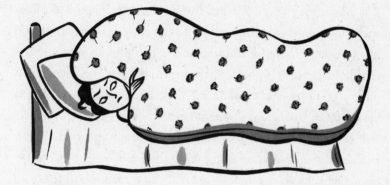

When I was once in the throes of a devastating breakup, my grandmother suggested that it was only a matter of time before I felt better. I, of course, thought that was easily the most useless piece of advice I had ever been given. I felt like I was grieving a death and wondered if, in fact, it was mine. Clearly, it seemed to me, Grandma, in her eighties, was completely out of touch with the realities of love. Looking back on it now, I realize that rarely have truer words been spoken.

In time, I did feel better. I wasn't exactly looking back and laughing, but the experience of heartbreak was a little like having a very bad cold. Once I felt better, it was difficult to really remember how miserable I had once felt. Unfortunately, I never got around to asking Grandma how, exactly, to pass the time from being crushed to feeling okay and better. But I have found my way back several times, as have my girlfriends, much to our amazement. And you will too.

This book is a synthesis of hundreds of hours that I have spent talking with friends in various stages of breakups, theirs and mine. It seemed to me that besides enormous telephone bills, there was a lot of advice shared that could be useful to others. The support of friends is one of the keys to recovery. But sometimes you can't reach your friends. They have lives and jobs, and maybe they live in a time zone that prohibits you from calling them when you are feeling your worst. So I decided to create a portable twenty-four-hour girlfriend with plenty of first- and secondhand experience and an organized approach to what is an insane process.

For example, if you find yourself in the middle of the night wondering if your ex was the One, before racing over to his house, check out the many reasons why a man who breaks up with you is actually disqualified from being the One. Or before picking up the phone to call your ex when you know it's probably not a good idea, why not glance at the reasons not to call him or at least look at the things to avoid if you absolutely have to go ahead? Or, if only to distract yourself from thinking about your ex, follow some of the suggestions on how to take care of yourself when you aren't feeling up to it. And why not consider some thoughts on how to move beyond blame, how to reclaim your vision of a life, and how to plug back in and make your life—and yourself—better than ever? And, if you are wondering how heavy an object you should throw at your ex if you run into him unexpectedly, look no further. Obviously something light enough—like an empty beer can—so that it will be practically impossible for him to press assault charges. It's good to have information like this at your fingertips, especially in the first stages of a breakup when your pride—and quite possibly your common sense—may have flown the coop.

When I sat down to write this book, I particularly had in mind women whose boyfriends had broken up with them. Naturally, there are times when it is equally painful to be the person initiating the split, and this book may be helpful to those of you in that position, especially if your ex basically broke up with you by behaving so badly that he forced you to say it's over. However, if what you are feeling is an overwhelming sense of relief and the urge to just get on with your life, there may still be a few tips of use to you.

The important things about living through a breakup are knowing you are not alone, retaining what dignity you can, not getting arrested, and eventually realizing that the best is ahead. I hope this book will help.

the girls' guide to
SURVIVING A
BREAKUP

QUIZ #1

Is it really a breakup?

This quiz can be helpful, but mostly it is a good way for you to distract yourself when you might otherwise be out keying your ex-boyfriend's car. It may make you feel better to see if your breakup is really legitimate.

Has the man in question ever asked you on a date?

If the answer is NO: I have a friend who imagines herself into relationships. I think the clinical term for it is erotomania. The more colloquial term for it is ridiculous, and this kind of behavior is guaranteed to make your friends want to change their phone numbers. If you have never been asked out by the person you feel is breaking up with you, you should seek professional help and fast. It is appropriate to feel disappointment when someone you are interested in does not seem interested in you—yeah, it hurts that he's started going out with someone else or never returned your call—but you are not in the throes of a breakup.

If the answer is YES: Read on.

Have you slept with him?

This is a tricky question.

If the answer is YES, but it turned out to be a one-night stand: If it feels like a big deal, first of all relax. Everyone, *everyone*, makes a few mistakes. Fire off a nasty note to the women who wrote *The Rules* and take a bubble bath. You didn't do anything wrong. It's not your fault that he turned out to be a total jerk. How were you to know? As a male friend pointed out to me, if a guy really likes you, he won't care that you slept with him right away. You are not in a breakup. I'm not saying that it's a great idea to sleep with a guy right away, but you never know where the chips are going to fall. Cheer up. You have a lot of company.

If the answer is YES, often: Read on.

If the answer is NO but you have been together for more than a month: Are you Amish? Read on.

If the answer is NO and you have known him for less than a month: An expensive haircut—including sexy highlights—and a few evenings out with your girlfriends talking about how guys suck should take care of the problem. If it doesn't, again you may want to seek professional help.

Were you together more than three months?

Three months may seem arbitrary. Of course, every relationship progresses at different speeds.

If the answer is NO: Most likely you are not really going through breakup hell. However, there are five fairly reasonable exceptions.

Exception #1: You knew your ex for a long time before you started going out.

Exception #2: You had the immediate feeling that this was the love of your life and you never wavered from that feeling during the time, albeit brief, that you were together.

Exception #3: All of your friends are in relationships and the thought of being alone again is extra-unbearable.

Exception #4: This breakup has brought back the trauma of a previous breakup that you are still grieving over and you just need a little extra guidance.

Exception #5: You are an exquisitely sensitive individual who finds the loss of any relationship heart-wrenching (i.e., you wept uncontrollably when your mailman moved to a new route).

If any of these apply: Read on.

If the answer is YES: Read on.

Did you live together?

Honey, if the answer is YES, definitely read on.

At this point, I have loosely defined what constitutes a real breakup and what just requires a cocktail and some shopping. For those of you still on board, let's get down to business.

1. the first few days: KEEP BREATHING

part one: MANAGING THE CRISIS

From the first moment that you have the wind knocked out of you by hearing in one way or another that the relationship is over, you must ruthlessly prioritize doing as little as possible. By that I mean you must accept that you are in shock and that you should expect nothing from yourself other than to keep breathing. Even that may seem like a stretch, but you can do it.

More than likely the breakup and the devastation you feel

were not anticipated. That's okay. Alert other people to the fact that for forty-eight to seventy-two hours nothing is about the most that they can expect from you, though not necessarily in those words. Take a half hour as soon as possible to clear the decks for two to three days so that you can fall apart with some dignity—and privacy.

IF YOU LIVE TOGETHER

While you may feel completely powerless at the moment of the breakup, keep in mind that your ex is more than likely feeling some guilt about upsetting you so. You must swiftly make use of this guilt to secure whatever you feel is going to be the most comfortable living arrangement for you for the next few days. You cannot enter the first hideous but necessary phase of a breakup until you are in a comfortable place away from your ex, so keep it quasi together for a few minutes to get this out of the way.

You may want to stay in your mutual abode. This has the added benefit of buying you some time to mark your name with a sharpie on as many of the joint acquisitions and CDs as you would like. When someone breaks up with you, it is more than reasonable to ask him to stay at a friend's or a parent's for a week, so even if your ex doesn't get this right away, know that you are well within your rights. If your ex is anything like the men I know, and you are crying, he will either want to go to bed with you or get the hell away from you. Do NOT sleep with him. It will not make you feel any better and it won't undo the breakup.

Once you have told him that he has to stay elsewhere for a little while, do not follow him around while he gets ready; do not hover. Be clear that you don't want to hear from him for a few days and that he may under no circumstances drop by. If you are feeling extremely untrusting and/or bitchy, you can ask him to give you his keys to the apartment—he probably will. Then give him exactly twenty minutes to gather what he will need and sequester yourself in another room and call a friend.

Of course, you may not want to stay at the place where you two lived together. You may feel oppressed by the reminders of your life together. If you are going to split, do it quickly. Do not drag your ass around moping. If you forget stuff, you can always borrow from whomever you are staying with. It's mature to let your ex know where you are going in case he needs to reach you in an emergency, i.e., the house burns down. You can tell him, but it's also wise to let him know that you would prefer he doesn't call you. You will contact him when you are ready. If you are feeling so pissed that you don't want to tell him where you are going, that's fine too. He has forfeited all rights to keep tabs on you.

SHARED PETS

This mostly comes up if you live together, though some people share pets without living together. Common sense dictates that, with rare exception, if the pet belonged to one of you coming into the relationship, it should leave the relationship with that person, even if it now feels as if the pet belongs to both of you. With a mutually acquired pet, if he has broken up with you, etiquette dictates that the choice is yours. So if you feel that having the pet around is going to make you feel better, keep it and say that in a month you will be willing to discuss a more joint arrangement. Don't leave the door open for a lot of contact around the pet anytime soon and don't use the pet as an excuse for contact. You need some time to start feeling better before you are in touch and certainly before you make any kind of permanent decisions about the pet. Of course, if you always hated the dog because it slobbered, or the cat because it shed, or the lizard just because, make him take it no matter how inconvenient it is for him.

You may worry that the pet will miss your ex. Don't. Remember that you are a little sensitive and emotional right now. Your pet will be getting a lot of love from you and will be happy giving you a lot of love. Keep in mind that your pet is not a person and, while sensitive, will make the best of the situation. Especially if you are the child of divorced parents, know clearly that your pet is not going through what you went through back then.

After her boyfriend left, my friend Hannah called me, crying, about how their dog, Rocco, was upset. Maybe Rocco was a little upset. Hannah sure was. Give yourself and your friends a break and try not to project too much of your own sadness onto the pet. I have never ever encountered a pet that didn't weather a breakup just fine. In hindsight, Rocco never had it better because Hannah started letting Rocco sleep on the bed and was home from work for a week snuggling with him.

WORK, OR GETTING OUT OF IT

Unless you are among the very lucky or very unlucky, you have a job. If your boss or your clients are cool, you can tell them that you and so-and-so are over and you need a few days to get yourself together. Be careful here. Most bosses and most clients are not cool, even though they pretend to be. Revealing any vulnerability may come back to haunt you later. If in doubt, lying is best.

Isn't this worse than a cold?

The best lie is, of course, calling in sick. You probably sound like shit anyway from crying. Take advantage of that and leave people voice mails, letting them know that you won't be in the next day. You will have bought yourself a day to call the next night and say you are still not feeling well and you'll keep them posted. If you decide to answer the phone during this period, be sure to sound as if you are dying.

To make matters easier, here are two really solid illnesses that can creep up on you unexpectedly and have unfortunate consequences but don't cause too much alarm. Pick your story and stick to it.

✿ The flu. This is a particularly useful choice if it happens to be fall or winter (and you don't live in the tropics). People spend those seasons chatting about how "it" is going around, and often the local media even gets in on the act. Why not you? I like this one because it's contagious and involves vomiting. As a result, people, even bosses, do not want you around. Be sure to complain of fever and chills.

✿ Food poisoning. This one lends itself most effectively to the spring and summer when you and others are more likely to be eating shellfish. Scallops, lobster, and shrimp are easy scapegoats. For those of you well known already to be allergic to shellfish, undercooked chicken and pork can come through in a pinch. Real food poisoning leaves you, at best, in a heap on your bathroom floor next to the toilet, not knowing which end of you is going to explode next. This choice means, of course, that no one but no one wants you to make an appearance in the office.

Short-Term Excuses

You have a few other lying options if you have used up all your sick days. If it's a Friday or a Thursday night and you need to get out of only one day of work, one of the following will do.

✿ A parent/sibling/close friend has thrown out her back and you are going to have to spend the day with her and take her to the doctor. It's not a great excuse, but it actually happened to me. Be sure to mention muscle relaxants and painkillers like Vicodin or Percoset.

✿ In many places, having your car break down can be prohibitive to working. This is good. Be careful, however, not to use this excuse too often because eventually it makes you look like a schmo. Be particularly careful if your job involves driving because overuse of this excuse could lead to unemployment.

Dramatic Excuses

If you have the most heartless boss or clients and you have taken a bunch of sick days or vacation recently, you may have to deliver a more dramatic excuse. Remember to stay focused on the fact that you need a few days off and do not use this situation as an opportunity to see if you really are a good actress. The following suggestions are to be used only as a last resort.

✿ Funeral time. Death in the family or of someone close to you. This is hideous. On the other hand, it could certainly buy you a whole week out of the office. Be careful to pick a person who is close enough to you that your life would be unhinged by his or her death but also distant enough that your office has never heard of this person. Never ever ever pick someone real.

This is guaranteed to bring you bad vibes and can also be awkward when that person calls your office in the future.

✿ Diagnosis of terminal illness. Not yours, dummy! Again, this is to be used only in extreme circumstances. The ill friend/family member has asked to stay with you for a few days. What could you say? Don't get caught up in any conversations focusing on what a brave and compassionate friend/relative you are. We both know the truth.

No Getting Out of It

Unfortunately, there are times when work cannot be avoided. Maybe you have an important presentation with colleagues from out of town, maybe you are a wedding planner and it's the big day. Whatever it is, denial of the breakup is the best way to go. Thank your now-ex for his input and get away from him so you can try to pretend he's just out of town. In the case of a presentation, make sure that you have everything you are going to say written down. With an event, come armed with to-do lists. Just focus on getting the work done so you can then move on to your breakdown. Keep in mind that it's fine if you do a lousy job. One bad performance will not in the long run ruin your career. When the work is done, do whatever you need to do to have a few days to yourself. If you need help, refer to the above suggestions.

This may not make you feel better right now, but there is a minuscule silver lining to the "have to work" scenario. It will come back to serve you later in the "anger" phase because you will have solid facts to support your theory that your ex is an ass. Anyone who breaks up with you during a work crunch surely sucks.

FRIENDS: REACHING OUT

As I've said, it's essential to get in touch with one or several close friends immediately. It is wise to call someone who is a very tolerant listener because you are not ready to have a real conversation just yet. For now, skip calling anyone who is going to lecture you on how he or she knew this would happen, or on how much of a jerk your ex was, or both. It is also best to call someone who won't mind if you are incapable of stringing together complete sentences, or if you are mostly just sobbing and dry heaving. If there isn't anyone this angelic in your circle of close friends, make your best choice. Also, if you can't reach the person you want to talk to, leave her a message to call you and then move on to calling other friends to keep yourself busy until your top choice calls you back. One important note, when leaving messages on friends' answering machines or if you are crying when you first get friends on the phone: However badly you are doing, try to croak out the words "broke up." Not to say that you are not in a serious crisis, but you don't want your friends to worry that a loved one has died, even if it feels a little that way.

Talking to friends is the very best tool you have in your own recovery, and you should make use of them and their love for you. You would do the same for them (if you wouldn't before, you will in the future), so do not feel bashful. They are sad that you are sad and they want to help you feel better. Ask them where they will be so that if you are a wreck you know where to find them. Check out the availability of several friends so you will almost always have someone to call and needn't rely on one person who, even if you are her favorite person in the whole world, probably has a few things that she needs to do. Take a piece of paper and write down when and where you can reach people for the next couple of days.

You may want to ask a friend to come and stay with you for a few days. If you do this, keep in mind that you should still keep up contact with a few other friends so the friend who is staying with you has time to do whatever she has to do (like go to work, perhaps) and stay sane so she can help you the best she can.

You may have decided to go stay at a friend's house. Bring your phone card or indicate that you will need to make a bunch of calls and ask if it is all right for you to pay her back later. No doubt this is fine with her. Again, it's good to stay in touch with other people while you are at your friend's house so she has time to take a shower, do laundry, and keep her life together. You don't want your friends to feel as if their lives are unraveling as well or they will not be very helpful to you.

A week should be enough time visiting a friend or having one stay with you to be able to function, at least in zombie-mode, on your own again.

PARENTS: HOW TO HANDLE?

Obviously, if you are estranged from your parents, or if they are abusive, leave them out of this. It is unlikely that someone who has disappointed you your whole life is suddenly going to come through for you right now, and you don't want to expose yourself to any additional hurt.

If your instinct is to call your parents right away, that is probably the right thing for you to do. Keep in mind that you may not be able to control how bad you sound, so here are a few things to consider before you pick up the phone.

Why Are You Calling Them?

You just want to tell them.

You may want to wait until you feel you can keep it together for the duration of the call. At least wait until you can get out a few complete sentences. Your parents, like most parents, are even more invested in you than your friends are. They care more, and your pain really is their pain. You don't want to panic them more than you are willing to involve them in your sadness. What I mean is this: If you call your parents when hysterical, you cannot expect them to be cool when you don't return their calls for a few days. You will have to take or return their calls relatively promptly, and you will have to keep them posted on how you are doing. If you don't, they may show up at your doorstep, and they would be right to do so. Do you really want them to race over and take you home and tuck you into your childhood bed? If this doesn't sound ideal, watch how despondent you sound when talking to them. Either way, I think it is good to let them know which friends you are in touch with, if you will be going to stay with any friends, or if you will have any friends staying with you. Remember, even though your ex broke up with you, and you are feeling horrible, this is not an opportunity to torment your parents unnecessarily.

You want to go "home."

If you feel that the best place for you to stay for a few days is with your parents, it probably is. It's a good idea to call and let them know what happened and that you are coming home. It's also a good idea, even if this doesn't ring totally true just yet, to say something like "for a few days" or "for the weekend." You want them to know that even though you sound like hell, you know that you will eventually get on with your life. In short, you want them to be prepared to let you leave their house again and go back to being a "grown-up" when you say you are ready.

A Cautionary Note

Even parents who are prone to being judgmental are probably capable of behaving appropriately for a few days when you are miserable. But if you think there is a chance that your parents are going to use the fact that you had your heart broken, probably by someone they didn't think was worthy of you, as an indictment of your bad judgment and your inability to function in the world as an adult, keep contact to a minimum. You shouldn't, and are not able to, defend your life right now. Wait until you've got your strength back. Also, if there is the remotest chance that your parents are going to take his side or try to blame you for the breakup, STAY AWAY. Sure, they may be worried that you have just broken up with the only gainfully employed man you've ever brought around and they just want you to be happy, etc., etc. Whatever their reasons, they are not going to give you the support you need right now.

SIBLINGS

If your siblings are abusive or judgmental, stay away from them during this time. If your siblings are crazy, this is also sound advice. My friend Josie would call her older brother Will, crying, every time someone broke up with her. Will would invariably race out, track the miscreant down, and punch him out. It was one thing when we were in high school, but it's not that funny anymore. Josie has spent a bunch of money on bail that could better have been used for massages, if she'd only called her brother when she was feeling less upset.

If you are lucky, siblings are like a cross between friends and parents. This means that you can generally count on them to be really cool and supportive. They are happy to hang out on the phone or pick up a six-pack and come over on a dime. This is great. The only thing to be careful about is that, a little like your parents, they are deeply affected by seeing you unhappy. They will want to be kept abreast of how you are doing and may get more protective of you in the future than you want them to be. Again, while it is probably a good idea to lean on them at this time, you may want to drop hints indicating that you know you will be feeling better soon and the like.

part two: FALLING APART SAFELY

Now that we have squared away how to get some peace and quiet for yourself, and whom to contact and how, let's move on to the brass tacks of dealing with an initial breakup. You are not yet ready to do a lot of loving things for yourself that will make you feel better and help you inch back toward your prebreakup level of self-esteem or better. You are probably feeling self-destructive. That's normal. This section is about passing some time safely.

DRUGS AND ALCOHOL

You know your limits better than I do, but we both know that your judgment probably isn't at its best right now. For myself, having several cocktails a few nights in a row in the wake of a breakup has been perfectly fine, even great. For you, this might be reckless or worse. So I'm outlining some don'ts and some general ideas that I hope will make you pause and think if you are making decisions about drugs and alcohol use.

Whatever choices you make, remember that it is completely normal for you to be in a lot of pain right now. Also keep in mind that in order to get through the pain, you have to feel it. This is NOT—thank god—an active process. Your brain is at work processing and accepting your heartbreak even as you are lying on the couch crying. But if you numb your brain with mind-altering substances for the next month, it won't perform its usual functions and you won't get any closer to feeling better.

Drugs

✿ Don't get behind the wheel of a car unless you are stone-cold sober. Even then, you are probably tired and blurry-eyed, so I recommend having someone else who is not in the middle of personal trauma chauffeur you around for a little while. Or take a cab.

✿ Don't take any drugs that have sketchy origins. You don't know what is really in there. You could be risking your life here. I can't say it firmly enough. This is *totally unacceptable* under any circumstances.

✿ Don't take any drugs you haven't tried before. This is not the time for experimenting.

✿ Don't take more than the recommended doses of any prescription drugs or any over-the-counter medicine you have around. As with any serious thoughts of suicide, if you feel yourself heading this way, take action NOW. You need to get professional help right away (see appendix). This is not the time to concern yourself with what other people might think or whether you yourself hold the ignorant belief that getting professional help makes you "crazy" or any less of a person. It doesn't matter. The most important thing is that when you are feeling horrible, you get yourself help. You will find later that it means that you are brave and smart and love yourself.

✿ Don't take any drugs if you have a history of drug abuse. You know this better than I do.

✿ Don't take any drugs when you are alone.

The Hard Stuff

Obviously there are a lot of different drugs out there that do different things. You may do none of them. You may do some of them but would never ever touch others. You may have tried many of them. What I'm saying is this: Don't do them now. What felt good when you were feeling good will most likely feel dramatically different when you are feeling terrible. And by different, I mean completely f—king horrible, horrible when you are on the drug, horrible when you are coming down, and potentially horrible for days after. If you have drugs around and you are concerned about taking them, give them away ASAP or literally flush them down the toilet immediately.

Alcohol

✿ Don't drive if you've had anything to drink, and probably don't drive anyway.

✿ Don't drink if you are a recovering alcoholic. Call your sponsor. You know this better than I do.

✿ Don't drink more than you usually do when alone. It can be dangerous.

✿ Don't mix your drinks. It's just never a good call.

For many reasons, even if you are not much of a drinker, you may feel moved to tie one on under the circumstances. Just keep in mind that your body isn't used to it. You will get the spins and very likely throw up. Even if you are a regular drinker, if you consume more alcohol than usual, you are going to get sick. I recommend not exceeding what you might do on any old Saturday night. You don't want to make yourself feel worse than you do ordinarily.

FOOD

Unless you have a history of eating disorders, there is probably very little that you can do on this front in forty-eight to seventy-two hours that is going to make much difference down the road.

Not Eating

When I am feeling incredibly hurt, I can barely eat. Normally I eat plenty, so if I'm consuming only Cool Whip and cigarettes for a few days, I don't worry about it. My appetite has never failed to come back when I am feeling better. But there are limits. If you haven't eaten anything for more than twenty-four hours, try to eat something. I find it best to force myself to eat a piece of toast or some pretzels. It doesn't really matter, but you don't want to eat so little that you start to make yourself feel light-headed and faint. If you are coming up on forty-eight hours and you still can't get yourself to eat something, you need to tell someone and get help.

Eating

While you don't want to make yourself feel sicker than you probably already do, feel free to indulge yourself in any cravings you have. One friend of mine likes to eat cartons of chocolate frozen yogurt out of the containers while sobbing. My friend Samantha's favorite man-hating meal is liverwurst and Swiss with tons of mustard. It doesn't matter. Eat whatever you want. Two or three days of it isn't going to affect your weight in the long run. Remember, takeout can be your best friend during this time of need.

WATER

You've been crying. Maybe you've been drinking. Maybe you are extremely hungover. Any which way, you should drink some water. Extreme dehydration probably isn't a serious concern, but even low-level dehydration will make you feel worse than you already do. Also your skin and hair need water to look their best. Do yourself a tiny little favor and drink a few glasses of water every day.

SMOKING

✿   If you are not a smoker: This is a bit dicey. I've seen several friends smoke a few or many cigarettes during the first few days of a breakup and drop it easily when they are feeling better. You know yourself better than I do. I will caution you that when I was nineteen, I had never smoked until my boyfriend dumped me while I was staying with him in Washington, DC. I had only one friend there, and she was having some serious problems of her own and was never around. It seemed comforting to have a few smokes. It reminded me of my girlfriends who were away for the summer. It's been twelve years now and I still haven't quit. It's not that I don't love smoking, but we all know that it's horrible for you. If you indulge during this time, try not to let it go on for more than a week because you could end up spending the next decade smelling like an ashtray.

✿ If you have recently quit: God, love you. I know it's rough, but if you can avoid starting again, you will be your own personal hero. If you do start, promise yourself that you have exactly one week to smoke and don't break that promise. He's just not worth destroying your tremendous accomplishment.

✿ If you are a smoker: Smoke on, baby. This is not the time to quit, and a few extra cartons aren't going to make it or break it with lung cancer. Sure, quitting could be in your nearish future, but another few weeks of smoking probably won't make any difference. If you decide, because you are superhuman, that you want to quit now, get help doing it because it's hard enough even without already feeling like hell.

EXERCISE

You may be one of those intimidating people who have to exercise every day and have been doing so for decades. In that case, you (a) frighten me and (b) should probably go sweat it out. But if you don't think you can handle it, that's totally cool too. A few days of skipping the gym won't make the slightest difference in the scheme of life or, more important, to your fine physique. If you are not prone to working out regularly, do not even think about forcing yourself to start now unless you are bizarrely moved to, as in an out-of-body experience. It can't hurt, but keep in mind that you are in a "no-pressure" zone.

MANILA ENVELOPES

You may use manila envelopes at work, but did you realize how handy they can be in a breakup?

Find everything that he's given you, or that belongs to him, or that reminds you of him, and put it in a manila envelope with his name written on it. This includes letters, printed out E-mails (if you have a lot of E-mails from him on your computer and aren't ready to lose them forever, print them out and then delete them all so you won't have to see them whenever you go to check your mail), photos, mix tapes, slim volumes of poetry. This process ensures that every time you turn around you won't see his face and also means, if you are as thorough as I am, that you won't be innocently going about your moping and stumble across that "love postcard" he wrote you when he was on vacation with his family in Florida. Then take everything that doesn't fit in a manila envelope, including that snuggly sweater, his boxers, the Kiss albums, and put it all in a garbage bag. Then shove the garbage bag in the back of a closet.

I find this activity extremely helpful, and it also helps pass the time. Of course, it can be a tad more challenging if you lived together. Obviously that hideous sofa will not easily fit in the envelope and you will need to plan some trips to the dump with your brother and his pickup.

You have now successfully ex-boyfriend-proofed your place. If you are like me, this means that you can now breathe a little easier.

SAFE PLACES

Imagine a place that is a safe happy place for you. It can be your grandmother's attic where you used to play with your cousin. It can be your fantasy of a thatched hut on a tropical beach as the sun is setting. Now, how does it smell? What is there besides you? A hammock, a quilt, a piña colada? Get acquainted with this place. And then go there in your mind whenever you start feeling panicky or overwhelmed with grief. Go there when you are sitting on the subway, when you are in a crowded elevator, when you are at home alone and feel as if you are falling apart. Stay there in your mind until you feel a little better.

Now pick your favorite place in your home. For me, it would have to be the bathroom with the bathtub running. For you, it might be sitting in your favorite chair by the window. And then decide that this is your safety zone. That means that when you go to that place, things are all right, things are going to get better. Nothing bad happens to you in that place. The next time you start feeling really bad, go to your safety zone. As many a late night infomercial will tell you, it's amazing how you can get yourself to feel better by using the power of your own mind.

OTHER ACTIVITIES

✿ Lying in bed in a fetal position. Sometimes you've just got to do nothing and be a miserable wretch. Try not to spend more than one complete day doing this. After twenty-four hours of said behavior, you should try to mix it up a little.

✿ Walking . . . for five minutes. You may not feel ready to get out of the house, but a superbrief walk around the block and a little fresh air might be a manageable break from sobbing on the couch. Be sure to go incognito—a hat and sunglasses will do.

✿ Movies. You may not feel up for going to the movies, but at least it's dark in there so no one can see your puffy eyes and red nose. Also, going to the movies during the day pretty much guarantees that you won't run into anyone you know since they are toiling at the office. (Sunglasses in theater optional.)

If you don't have a VCR or DVD, I feel for you. You should

try to get your hands on one right away. Forcing yourself to watch and possibly cry through movies is very therapeutic. Of course, avoid movies that are going to remind you of him and make you feel even worse. Anything tragic and all serious dramas are out. This is not the time to see if *Kramer vs. Kramer* was as harsh as you remember. Stupid comedies are good and so are golden oldies.

Watch my recommended movies from the list on the next page, watch some other movies. It doesn't really matter. Just force yourself to sit through a few movies, and inevitably time goes by.

✿ TV. It is essential to watch a lot of TV—especially bad TV—when you feel that the bottom has fallen out.

CONCLUSION

More than likely, you are not capable of doing much beyond what I've suggested in this chapter during the first few days following a breakup. If you feel you can do more, you are doing better than me and all my friends and you can move ahead to the suggestions in the next chapter. If you can't, don't worry. The complete emotional turmoil of what you are going through right now will pass. My friend Hannah, when she was really bottoming out, said to me that she wished she could just be in a coma for a month. But she and I both knew that being in a coma wouldn't really help. She would wake up from it as tortured as she was when she conked out. You just have to live through these dark days. That's it. And if you can just hold on, you will feel better despite yourself.

Top 5 Movies to Distract You

1. *Airplane*: This is one of the funniest movies of all time. Whether you speak jive or not, it's sure to crack at least a smile.
2. *Nine to Five*: The only problem with this classic is that the theme song is so infectious you may never get it out of your head. The combination of Dolly Parton, Jane Fonda, and Lily Tomlin is pure joy.
3. *Private Benjamin*: Who can resist Goldie Hawn's goofy charm? And, as my friend Emily pointed out, you may have it bad but at least you don't have Captain Doreen Lewis breathing down your neck.
4. *The Thin Man*: This is one of my favorite movies of all time. The only old-fashioned thing about it is the extraordinary amount of booze consumed by Nick and Nora Charles. William Powell and Myrna Loy are perfect in this dynamite combination of comedy and mystery. You won't find wittier dialogue anywhere.
5. *Fletch*: Yeah, you've forgotten about this treasure because you've probably forgotten that Chevy Chase was ever funny. But he was, and nowhere was he funnier than here. Check it out.

Top 5 TV Shows to Distract You

1. *Magnum, PI*: It was great then, and nothing has changed. That's because it's all reruns.
2. *Charlie's Angels*: Not the movie, silly! Yeah, they're somewhere inside your TV in reruns. Find them. Whatever trio you tap into, remember that the girls are your friends.

3. *Friends* **and** *Seinfeld*: Not my personal favorites, but everyone else likes them so maybe you do too. I think collectively they are on about seventeen times a day, so if you can use your remote control you should be able to watch them.

4. *Ally McBeal*: I am not a big fan of this show, but if your mind is not already numb from pain, this should do the trick. Also, Ally is always getting dumped.

5. *Sex and the City*: I watch this show and I like it a lot. My brother thinks it's offensive to women. As I pointed out, however, not half as offensive to women as when he sleeps with them and doesn't call them again. Anyway, it's about four broads with a taste for expensive accessories, doing trendy things in New York, who are chronically dealing with breakups. There's at least one breakup per episode. But it's smart and lighthearted. If you don't have premium cable, this may be the time to spend that $12.95 per month.

QUIZ #2

Do You Need a Straitjacket?

I'm sure you don't, but you may feel as if you do. Here are a couple questions to help you check in with your mental health. Whatever your answers, you should high-five yourself that you are reading this and not out buying a gun.

Are you sleeping more than twelve hours a day?

If the answer is NO: Read on.

If the answer is YES: Don't be alarmed. Oversleeping may just be the way you cope with emotional turmoil. Frankly, it's not the worst way you could go. But if it continues for another week and you are feeling as if you can't wake up, you're probably wading into the murky waters of clinical depression. That's pretty common around heartbreak, but you may want to reach out and get some help.

Are you not sleeping at all?

If the answer is NO: Read on.

If the answer is NO but you are not sleeping well and/or that much: Trouble sleeping is an extremely common side effect of breaking up and probably isn't that big a deal unless it goes on for weeks and you aren't able to deal with whatever you need to deal with—like work or feeding the dog. Josie was really upset about going to bed alone after her boyfriend left and, as a result, she would do anything to avoid going to bed. After a few weeks of this, she got so tired of being tired she started putting herself to bed again and getting regular shut-eye. So if that's what is going on, you will probably correct the situation on your own when you are feeling a little better.

If the answer is YES: If you are not sleeping at all—and by that I mean not even a couple of hours a night—you should probably get help. In college, Samantha and I learned that humans actually go crazy if they don't sleep. Samantha's boyfriend—a complete ass—broke up with her during final exams. Understandably, Samantha was a wreck. She didn't really sleep well anyway, so she decided to pull some all-nighters—no sleep at all. I came back from class on the third day and found Samantha standing under a tree outside her room trying to get her "edges straight" so she could properly ski over some imaginary moguls. It was May in New Jersey. I started talking to her and slowly realized that she thought she was in Vermont on Christmas break. It took a while to convince the doctor at the infirmary that Samantha wasn't on any drugs, but eventually he believed me and, after sleeping for sixteen hours at the infirmary, Samantha was back to her usual self. You probably want to avoid something like this happening to you.

Are you drunk or high before 5 P.M.?

If the answer is NO: Read on.

If the answer is NO but you spend your evenings getting blotto: You thought you were going to get off easy with the 5 P.M. thing. Not so fast, baby. A few nights of having one too many may be all right—for a few nights only—but you want to be very honest and very careful here that things don't get unhealthy.

If the answer is NO but you usually wake up around 4:53 P.M.: If you haven't been sober for at least eight hours before you hit the sauce, the flag is up and you should change your answer to YES and see below.

If the answer is YES: Honey, passing your days in the company of Jack Daniel's is absolutely NOT OKAY. Look, if it's Saturday and your best friend came over and you had a few mimosas and got tipsy, fine. But if your days are spent in a fog of drugs or alcohol, you need to get help. This breakup may be excruciating, but no man, nothing, is worth behaving this self-destructively.

Have you still not showered?

If the answer is NO: Read on.

If the answer is YES: If you haven't showered in more than three days, you need to put this book down immediately and take a shower. And while you are in there, wash your hair. If you can be trusted with sharp objects, shave. It's one thing to be depressed. It's quite another to be depressed and nasty.

If after a week you are answering yes to more than one of these questions, you may need some bonus help. Don't freak out, but take a break from reading and make an appointment to get help soon. See the handy numbers in the appendix.

2. the first month beyond the first few days:
SLOWLY GETTING A GRIP

part one: THE RELATIONSHIP, YOU, AND HOT TOPICS

Most of you should start to feel less worse around now. You
have made it through the first few days! You may not feel good,
but you are not completely out of your mind. While there are
going to be difficult times ahead, the very worst is over. The
good news: Now that you are not loco, there is a lot more that
you can do for yourself. The bad news: You are no longer in
shock and over this next month you will be facing the reality

that the relationship is really over. It will probably hit you at random times more acutely than at others, though you will probably be conscious of the loss throughout. Still, you are right where you need to be to start coming back to being better than ever.

I've broken down this chapter into two sections. The first section discusses issues that relate to the relationship. Obviously, you are still thinking about it and him a lot. The second section is designed to help you start shifting the focus onto your own recovery and well-being. I split the chapter up this way so it isn't too confusing, but you need to be balancing both the past and the present, so feel free to skip around.

HE IS NOT THE ONE

I want to get this out of the way right now. You are going to be thinking a lot about what happened to make him think that the relationship should end. That's fine. If the man you have been with is anything like the men I've known, he probably left you with a lot more questions than answers. But through all your thinking and talking, I want you to remember one thing: In the simple act of breaking up with you, he has proved himself to NOT be the One for you. That may seem obvious to you, and if it does, you are doing great. I, however, have spent precious hours wondering if the guy who left me was supposed to be the father of my children, the man I was supposed to walk into the sunset with. I have also spent a lot of time talking with heart-broken girlfriends about whether they somehow lost the love of their life just after he slammed the door on his way out.

You may wonder what you could have done differently, what was wrong with you, what was wrong with the relationship. All of these things may be interesting for you, your friends, or a high-priced psychiatrist to consider. You want to learn something through this wretched process, if possible, and you want to prepare yourself to have the best future relationships you can. But I think it is really worthless to wonder if the one who left was the One. He disqualified himself just by breaking up with you. Here are the main two reasons that I feel this way:

✿ Life is hard. It's not hard every second of every day, but harsh shit happens. You lose your job. Your parent dies. You are broke. Your friend dies. You are sick. You are trying to be a good parent and you are working. Your child is sick. Someone you know gets into a car accident. You have a miscarriage. In the course of your life, most of these things will happen to you. You will live through them, but if you want to have a man at your side, he has to be a man you can count on who will not head for the door when the going gets tough. Unless you've been going through a really difficult patch lately, the guy who just broke up with you hasn't seen nothin' yet and already he's gone. So, he's not the One.

✿ You may think you've lost the best thing you've ever had and so you are really down. Know this: You haven't. Take Samantha's sister, for example. She was living with a man for five years when he upped and dumped her. She was in her late thirties and devastated. If the guy who had wanted to live with her for all that time and had professed that he loved her didn't want to be with her, who would? Well, the man she just married, who is light-years smarter, kinder, taller than her ex. Just because your ex doesn't want to be with you doesn't mean that another man won't, and it doesn't mean that your ex is the best man you'll find. Life just doesn't work that way. You may be kicked to the curb by a big loser and discover in the near future that a really wonderful man would weather any storm to be with you.

My point is that until you are with the One, he's still in your future. The One is never the guy in your past, or he wouldn't be in your past. You just can't get dumped by the One.

WHY DID IT HAPPEN?

In my experience, there are three main reasons why a person breaks up with you. You may recognize them from times that you have been sitting on the other side of the table.

He's Not in Love with You

I know it's horrible. If this is what he said, I just want you to know that I can't believe it either, and I think he's a fool. Unfortunately, there isn't much that you can do with this one. On the other hand, when you are talking about men—and I've done this before, though not as well as my friend Holly who really is a genius at it—you can easily move away from the "he's not in love with you" scenario to "he's f—ked up."

He's F—ked Up

No matter how great you thought he was, he probably is f—ked up. It may not be the reason he broke up with you, or it might be. In the end, it doesn't really matter what the reason is, so if it makes you feel a lot better to think that he's actually in love with you but can't have a real relationship because his father split when he was a kid or whatever, fine. The only thing that I'd caution you about here is not to waste too much time or creative energy that could be spent doing something healing, contemplating ways that he's f—ked up and hence can't be with you.

You may not have to be very inventive at all. He may clearly be a mess. It may almost be comical what a basket case he was even though you loved him. And it may be helpful to talk to your friends about how many problems this guy had. It may be helpful in the anger phase and it may help you walk away because you probably are better off without him. Someday you may even want to thank him for letting you go. All this is fine. But if it's not apparent how messed up and inappropriate this man is for you, don't push it.

Keep it clear in your mind that this is no time for empathy. He broke up with you. You must untrain yourself from being supercompassionate about his problems or even from thinking about them too much. Everyone has problems, some of them even serious, and yet most of us still manage to stay in our relationships. If you want to feel compassion for someone, then direct it at yourself. He hurt you.

Let's get back to Holly for a moment. Holly has never ever had someone break up with her who wasn't actually madly in love with her but, because of some sob story, couldn't be with her. Now, Holly has dated some really unfortunate men, and it's true that they have had a lot of personal problems that could easily explain why they couldn't be in healthy relationships. In fact, that is its own fairly serious problem, and it might be yours too. It has been mine as well as every woman's—at least at some point—so don't get too worked up. You are in good company, and this is something you can work on. But when faced with a breakup, Holly will, for weeks if not months, roll around in her head and talk to friends about everything that ever happened to her ex as an excuse for him breaking up with her. She seems unable to get away from feeling sorry for the jerk and just get pissed. I can't tell you how many nights I have spent listening to her dissect the high school angst of a man in his midthirties who has recently broken her heart. It's not pretty, and oftentimes I feel like a bad friend when I stay on the phone and indulge her. It just doesn't matter how depressed or unhappy your ex is or has been unless it's in relation to why you would be with someone who has so many problems. From this point on, the only interesting thing about your ex's problems is what it says about *you* that you would tolerate them.

Also, be careful with your friends here. Keep in mind that your ex is already on their shit list. At first, they may be open to discussing his problems in a somewhat sympathetic way. Don't be fooled. They are letting you carry on this way only because they love you and they figure it's better for you to be on the phone with them than doing something silly. After a few weeks, they are still going to be willing to talk about how much your ex sucked, but only when it has no overtones of pity. After all, they are not talking to you about him because they care about him. Make no mistake. Unlike you, they were never in love with him. They are talking to you about all this stuff only because they care about you. There are plenty of messed-up people out there for them to get teary-eyed about who have not recently crushed one of their favorite people on the planet.

If you are unable to stop analyzing you ex's problems and start taking great care of yourself, you may have self-esteem damage that predates this relationship and is holding you back. This is extremely common and you may want to try professional help.

He's Not Ready for Commitment

This is a very handy excuse that men use to get out of relationships, and they are not afraid to use it until way beyond an age that is appropriate. Really, the only upside to this excuse is that you should feel free to use it if you're ever in a relationship you want out of and can't think of anything more compelling. The truth is that in our culture "readiness for commitment" has become a big issue, bigger than ever before, for both men and women. Why? Obviously the effects of the sexual revolution, the economic changes of last fifty years, and the me generation are complicated, but here is a quick sketch.

Before the 1960s, it was basically assumed, though it didn't always play out this way, that boys would grow up to be fathers and providers. They would marry early in their careers or while still in school, and everyone hoped that things would work out for the best. Women might or might not work, but either way—even if it was a myth—their work wasn't regarded as essential to a marriage or a family. And in the past, one person working might actually have been enough to support another adult and some munchkins. For some, life may be still like this.

But many single men I've spoken to don't feel they should take on the responsibilities of marriage and possible fatherhood until they've achieved some level of accomplishment in their professional lives, the level that it would take in this day and age to support a whole family. And that can mean delaying marriage or even committing to a real relationship for a long time. I think that many of these men will not really feel they should be more advanced in the relationship department, wherever their careers are taking them, until they hit forty or so and realize they aren't so young anymore. Sure, this delay could also just mask the fact that they are f—ked up, but while the whole "readiness to commit" thing wasn't culturally acceptable before, it is now.

In my experience, my female friends view relationships more fluidly or more romantically. If a relationship is really great, they don't hesitate to stick with it, wherever they are professionally. They may get freaked out about having kids but generally not about being in a serious relationship or even getting married. Additionally, the most pragmatic women I know don't imagine that their careers, even if it's possible, will have to support an entire family. So they can feel a bit more relaxed. Finally, by and large, the women I know start feeling as if they should be getting serious about relationships in their early thirties, partially because of societal pressure, partially out of wanting to have a close loving relationship, partially out of noticing how little time they have left to have children if they want to have children.

Often, it seems that problems arise around "readiness for commitment" because single men and single women are generally dating people around their own age. You might think that women should date men ten years their senior and men should date women ten years their junior but, from what I've observed, they just don't. On some level, they feel most comfortable with people their own age and, with few exceptions, time and again seek out members of the opposite sex within a few years of themselves.

Another big issue for men—and women—is that people are far more concerned with "finding themselves" or "happiness" than ever before. While this might not seem as if it would create friction in terms of people committing themselves to relationships (why not find yourself with someone else hanging around?), it sometimes does. It seems that individual personal happiness has become *the* goal, and with all the confining roles that past generations have been forced into, it seems normal that a lot of men and women want to take advantage of new freedoms. Here problems seem to arise when men and women mistake the regular compromises that are the inevitable result of being in a close relationship or a marriage or a family with compromising their individual happiness. If a man makes this mistake, you've got to question if being in a close relationship even fits into his idea of happiness, because I can tell you from experience that there is no close romantic relationship that doesn't involve some compromise, even when it is the best thing that ever happened to you.

So where does this leave you? Just where you might expect: having to face the reality that this relationship is over. When someone isn't ready to commit to being with you when you are ready to commit to being with him, it's not going to work. He may be caught up in huge societal and cultural forces, or he may be a mess, but don't be alarmed. Most people—men and women—actually do want to be in a close, loving relationship with someone around their age, wherever they are financially and with their quest for personal happiness. You may get ridiculously lucky next time and find yourself involved with someone who already has everything worked out. More likely you will find yourself with someone who doesn't know how everything is going to turn out, but wants you—with your own uncertainties about who you are going to be—along for the ride.

THE WEE HOURS

"Then I thought of her walking up the street and stepping into the car, as I had last seen her, and of course in a little while I felt

like hell again. It is awfully easy to be hard-boiled about everything in the daytime, but at night it is another thing."

—Ernest Hemingway, *The Sun Also Rises*

It may seem inappropriate to quote a macho male writer in a
book for women about getting dumped, but there's no getting
around the fact that Hemingway nailed it here. Most of you are
going to do better during the day than you do at night, particularly the later at night it gets. You've probably already noticed
this phenomenon. It's just true that the wee hours are harder
and we're going to have to work with that. One simple but beautiful thing to remember is that no matter how bleak the middle
of the night seems, dawn is on its way and can't be stopped.

Don'ts

❀ *Do Not Call Him*

Whether or not you should contact him in general is a larger
issue that I address later, but it's never a good idea to call him in
the middle of the night. (For these purposes, the middle of the
night is any time from 11 P.M. to 8 A.M.)

There's a brilliant cartoon of a woman with her hair standing on end, surrounded by Kleenex, with a phone in her hand
getting an electric shock. The clock on the wall behind her
shows it's 3 A.M. The caption reads something like: "The Phone
Shocker: Perfect for Stopping You From Making Those
Embarrassing 3 A.M. Phone Calls That You Will Regret!" I
haven't been able to find this gadget in real life, but if you are
anything like me or my friend Lucy, it could come in real
handy.

Lucy will keep you on the phone for hours going over why

she is not-not-not going to call her ex even though she is dying to do it. Eventually she will say the coast is clear and she is going to bed. By now it's usually around 3 A.M. She will hang up the phone with you. She will then wait about five seconds and call him. He will be sleeping (surprise!), and their conversation will inevitably be disappointing to Lucy. She will then freak out for a few hours, smoking a carton of cigarettes, and call you back hysterical at the crack of dawn. While this is a very common scenario and I've played it out myself several humiliating times, it's not good. I have never ever known anyone who has felt better after a wee hours phone call to her ex than she did before. It's unlikely that you are going to be the first.

Also, it is quite possible that your judgment is not so great right now because not only are you tired and emotionally strung out but maybe you've had a few cocktails or a few brewskis. Here's the deal: NEVER DRINK AND DIAL.

✿ *Do Not Send That E-Mail*

I think I may be too old to think of E-mail as a way of conveying urgent emotion. Or, more likely, it's just that I got married before I even had a personal E-mail account. Sure, I had interoffice E-mail during several breakups but, really, what purpose would it have served to send my colleague in the next cubicle a passionate E-mail about a man she'd never met? However, I try to stay hip to what's happening, especially with my friends, and I know there's a lot of E-mailing going on out there that is romantic and even heartbroken in nature. And I think that's totally cool. Writing can be very therapeutic, and often it's easier to convey your thoughts when someone is not interrupting you every two seconds. In my day, that's what writing letters and sending them FedEx was all about. So if you find yourself in the middle of the night writing out a ton of thoughts to your ex via E-mail, you are not entirely in the wrong. In fact, write your heart out. The key thing is, DO NOT PRESS "SEND." Print the E-mail in question and put it in the "Send Later" bin. Sure, you can reread your E-mail a million times and edit it to perfection, but your judgment this late at night and this hurt is not 100 percent no matter what the tequila is telling you. You can do yourself zero, nada, no harm by holding on to your electronic missive until you've managed to sleep a few hours and look at it again and/or have had the chance to read it to a friend.

✿ *Do Not Go Over to His House*

This is like the "don't call him" situation only ten times more horrible. It's upsetting me just thinking about you dragging your bed-head self over to his house and standing there in front of his door, sad and only about to get sadder. It's not even that I care that he's going to think you are psycho and tell all his friends about your "visit," it's just that this kind of behavior means that you aren't loving yourself as much as you should.

✿ *Do Not Go Out for a Walk*

If it's still dark out and the streets are basically empty and you live in a neighborhood where there is the potential for crime—which means anywhere on this planet—this is not a good idea. Maybe your hands are a registered weapon. Perhaps you are the baddest bad-ass marine in town. Any way you look at it, this is no time to chance it. With you being female and reality being what it is, it is just plain stupid to put yourself at any kind of risk—now, because you are probably not at your most alert, or ever, really.

Do's

✿ *Call a Friend Instead of Calling Him*

This is flawless operating procedure. At this point in Lucy's story, she was doing great. When you think you might call him, especially if it is already pretty late at night, you must call a friend instead. If that friend isn't home or is asleep, call someone else and keep going until you get someone on the phone. It's handy to know that your bank, your credit card company, customer service at J. Crew (not a good idea if you are already saddled with major debt) are all available twenty-four hours a day, and generally you won't spend four hours on hold if it's the middle of the night. These are poor substitutes for a good friend but, in a crisis, they can be distracting (see Top 5 Web Sites). As a friend, before we got off the phone, I should have made Lucy promise me that she would not call her ex that night and that we would reconvene on this issue the next day. While a promise to a friend in the middle of the night may not seem to carry much weight, it has made me hesitate, at least for a few hours, when I was about to do something stupid. If your friend doesn't ask you to make her a promise, ask her to make you promise not to call him until at least the next day.

✿ *Go to Your Friend's House*

You might hesitate to ask this kind of favor from a friend, but believe me it is much much better than going to his house or going for a walk. If you are feeling really low, you will probably feel better lying on some else's couch watching TV (particularly if she has premium cable), even if she's gone back to bed. It's wise to call in advance so your friend knows that you are en route and you know that she is home.

✿ *Write Him a Letter (But Don't Even Think of Sending It Right Away)*

Write your ass off on paper. If you feel you have to write E-mail-style, as I've covered, print it out but do not send it. Write through your tears. Curse him out. Tell him what you really think of his family. Say anything and everything that comes to mind. Yeah, you faked it, he's small, whatever. This is your time to completely lash out and let down your guard. This is an excellent exercise. And maybe you will eventually hit the "send" button or drop the letter in the mail. But do not even think about doing that until you've gotten some sleep and reread it, and/or read it to a friend who really is your ally and have been given the okay by him or her.

❧ *Counting Sheep Is Silly But . . .*

Of course, it would be best if you were sound asleep and more convenient if you were at your own house. But if you can't sleep, don't get upset about it. You will only make yourself feel worse and it won't make it any easier to get to sleep. Keep in mind that a sleepless night here and there is not the end of the world and will probably ensure that you will sleep okay the next night. If you are worried that you will not be able to go to work in the morning, relax. I've had tons of sleepless nights and managed to do what I had to do the next day. You can too. So maybe you cut out of the office a few hours early the next day, so what. You'll be just fine. If you have more than two nights when you can't sleep at all, call your doctor. Insomnia is extremely common, breakup or no breakup, and your doctor should have a lot of ways to help you get some shut-eye.

In the meantime, don't lie there tossing and turning and freaking out.

✿ Get up and take a hot bath. Bring some magazines in there for good measure. Just be careful not to fall asleep in the tub.

✿ Sit up in bed and read a book. It seems too easy, but this has knocked me out many a time.

✿ TV and movies can come in handy here as well. Just sit there and force yourself to watch. Even though this isn't a good long-term solution, you will eventually pass out.

✿ Go on-line. See who's chatting at this ungodly hour. Check out the ridiculous things people are selling on eBay.

CONTACTING HIM IN GENERAL

You are probably going to feel the urge to do this at some point around now. I don't recommend it, but even the most stoic of my friends haven't managed to avoid doing it. Other fairly reasonable people have suggested that contacting him can be a good thing. Let's break it down.

Should You Call Him?

✿ *You miss him. You want to hear his voice. Mostly you hope that he is miserable too and that he still loves you and realizes this whole thing is a big mistake.*

The harsh reality is that he has a phone too. If he wants to call you, he can and will. If, for some reason, you've changed your number, he can get you at work. Know this: He probably does miss you, he probably is miserable, but he probably doesn't want to get back together, or he would be in touch. If these are the reasons you want to call him, don't. It'll only make you feel worse.

✿ *You are trying to figure out the relationship.*

This is a little bit trickier. Is what he says really going to help you understand things better? Is it going to make you feel better? Or are you going to rehash the same old stuff and be back where you started just when you were doing a little better? Occasionally, after a breakup and after at least two weeks of self-restraint, if you can be calm, you may be able to call your ex and have a productive, semiamicable call. He's feeling more relaxed than he was when you were together because there are no more expectations and, by waiting a few weeks, you've disarmed him into thinking that you can have a rational conversation about the relationship and the breakup. And maybe you can. But is this really going to be enough? If you have a good talk where he tells you some things that you didn't understand or never knew, are you going to be able to keep it straight that in no way does that mean you are going to get back together? Is the information you gleaned going to outweigh the hurt you will feel when you get off the phone and realize that you are still broken up? Also, do you really want to lull him into feeling that he can call you casually, as if you are now buddies? Only you really know. Try to stay honest with yourself. You are the one who is going to be hurt by trying to be bigger or stronger than you really are.

❧ *You have to tell him something.*

Look, you and I both know that this is bullshit. If his friend calls your place looking for him, if you find his prescription for Prozac, if he gets some mail at your place, if you notice his favorite antique car is for sale on eBay for $2.99, if his boss calls looking for him, etc. Cry me a river. You do not need to call him to tell him. If he is concerned that you have some of his stuff or some mail, he can call you. Furthermore, part of this dreadful process is stopping yourself from doing nice, thoughtful things for him. If he has broken up with you, you are not going to win him back by being a martyr, and it's going to make you feel, without exception, bad.

✿ *You think he's the only person who can make you feel better.*

When someone hurts you emotionally, it's human nature to feel that only that same person can heal you. But consider this: If someone broke your arm, you wouldn't ask him to treat you for it. You'd go to a doctor. I'm not saying that you need a doctor. I'm just saying that your ex cannot help you heal, as he is the one inflicting your pain. You are the only person who can make yourself feel whole again, so I recommend you leave him out of this.

Whatever you decide, here are some things not to do:

✿ As I've covered, calling in the middle of the night is not okay. Even though it may seem totally urgent, if you can hold on for a few minutes and consider how he's going nowhere and that, if you still feel you need to, you can call him the next day, you may start to feel a bit calmer. I am not lying. Repeat: He is going nowhere and nothing is going to change between now and tomorrow. If you are afraid that you are going to forget your urgent point, write it down and read it in the light of day to make sure it makes sense.

✿ Calling him at work. This, again, is really not a good idea. You don't want him to be any more hostile than he might be on hearing from you, and calling him at work practically guarantees that his back will be up. Even if he is a really nice person and happy to talk to you, calling him at work means he will be unable to talk as comfortably or as long as he might if you spoke to him at home.

✿   Calling him when you are drunk. Do not drink and dial. Obviously it is all right to be sipping your first glass of Chardonnay, but when you are sloppy, stay away from that phone.

✿   Calling him in the morning as he is getting ready for work. Again, if you are going to call, you want to have as much going for the conversation as possible. Catching him when he is groggy and/or in a hurry is not going to help.

✿   Calling early in the morning on the weekend. Unless he's one of those early bird types, this could be perceived as hostile and get you off on the wrong foot. If he's like many men, you should probably also avoid calling during a major sporting event like the Super Bowl. You don't need to seem like a dingbat.

If You Are Going to Call Him

✿   Call him at home. If you've tried him three times and he's never home, leave a calm message saying you'd really like to talk and could he call you at his convenience. This is the classy thing to do, though it means that you have to wait a while (I hope you decide to wait forever) before calling again if he doesn't return your call.

✿   Call at a reasonable time.

✿   From a conversation content perspective, perhaps the most important thing is to have a few clear things that you'd like to discuss. You don't need to get carried away with a typed-up agenda, but it's good to have a few questions/topics and to have thought through the phrasing of them if you actually want answers. For example, a question like, "You stupid, ungrateful bastard, how the hell did you expect me to be supportive about your new job when I'm busy working my ass off making twice what you do?" might leave you listening to the dial tone when you could approach it more like this: "I know you mentioned that you thought I wasn't supportive enough about your new job, and I'm sorry that you felt that way. I hope you realize that this was largely because I felt so overwhelmed with my own responsibilities at work." Then see what he says. Also, saying up front that you had a few things that you hoped you two could talk about may put him, however deceptively, at ease so he won't worry, at least at first, that you are about to bring up every aspect of the whole relationship and start crying and screaming. Again, though, what is he going to say that makes any difference?

Should You E-Mail Him?

My thoughts here are basically the same as on calling. Why are you contacting a man who doesn't want to be with you? He's not going to get back with you because you are a good writer. He could E-mail you if he wanted to be in touch or, alternately, he could show up at your house with flowers and crying if he really wanted to get back on board. He hasn't, so what is the point?

LISTS ARE YOUR FRIENDS

This may seem silly, but lists can really help you during this month when you are still thinking about him a lot and have many thoughts to sort out. They also waste time and, while perhaps still focused on the relationship, encourage some measure of being proactive.

Types of Lists

As Samantha, who recently went through a breakup, pointed out, the best list under the circumstances is the list of things that, despite your grief, you are psyched you won't have to deal with anymore. In her case, the list included her ex's porn collection, his horrible sister, his parents' depressing retirement community, her ex's awkwardness in social situations, his two left feet, his tighty-whiteys. You get the drift. Samantha said that her list was so long that even though she was so sad, she actually started to feel a bit relieved. You have nothing to lose by giving this a whirl.

Another good list is all the things that were wrong with the relationship. This list can be both helpful for future relationships and can make you feel a little relieved. Even the best relationship has some of these, so if you can't think of anything, you are probably not trying very hard. Some of the things I've included in the past are not having enough interests in common, he didn't like spending time with my friends, I didn't like his friends, he never told me what he was thinking, he made me feel like I was too emotional, I never was that attracted to him, he was dumber than me, etc. This list can help you figure out things that you need to avoid in the future and things that you need to work on and be more tolerant of.

A very important list that can help you to start feeling a little better about yourself is of things you like about yourself. If you have trouble with this list, it's fine to ask other people to remind you about the things that make you great. It can include physical attributes (the beauty mark on my cleavage, the fact that I can do a backbend), to the professional (I'm great on the phone, I know QuickBooks Pro inside out), to the emotional (I was a good friend to Jane when her brother passed away, I love my cat), to the random (I make great cupcakes, I can dance the Charleston). It doesn't matter what the things are that you like about yourself.

It matters that you can, with or without help, think of twenty or more things that remind you that you are snazzy.

CURIOSITY KILLED THE CAT—BEWARE

Sometime during this month, depending on how you are doing, you are going to start having devious thoughts. That's totally normal. As you might expect, it's best not to act on them. If you do, just keep in mind that you are not going to feel better. Almost every woman has acted out a few sneaky maneuvers at some point around a breakup. However, I almost think it would be better to call and scream at him in the middle of the night than to start snooping around.

Josie knew how to check her boyfriend's voice mail at home. She never checked it until he ended things. Then she started checking it compulsively. She learned that he had started dating an old girlfriend of his. She interpreted the old girlfriend's familiar messages as a sign that her ex had been seeing his old flame before they even broke up. Josie will never know. But she was devastated. As her friend, I realized that it would have been better if she had exhausted herself trying to get to the bottom of why things didn't work with her ex directly than to be spying on him. She was under the impression that it was somehow more humiliating to call him than to eavesdrop on his life. She was wrong. While I think calling her ex would have made her feel vulnerable and he might have thought she was extremely hurt, she was both of those things. Checking his voice mail left her with more questions than answers, made her feel like a big loser, and left her with a level of distrust for men that haunts her to this day, based on a suspicion that she will never confirm.

You may know how to check your ex's E-mail, voice mail,

mail. Don't do it. Very likely you will find something upsetting. In fact, anything may seem hurtful to you around this time. You may be devastated that he's going to a ball game with his friend, or that a female colleague of his called to ask him a work question. You don't need any more fodder to fuel your sadness. Aren't you feeling bad enough?

Snooping may even lead to discovering something potentially horrifying, as it did for Josie. But like Josie you will probably be too embarrassed to ask him about it, and it will leave you feeling much worse than before. Or, on the other hand, you may confront him about whatever you learn. Nine times out of ten it won't amount to anything and you will feel like a fool. And the tenth time? So he is doing something that is truly horrible, does it make you feel better to know? He's already out of your life, and the next guy you are with is going to be a whole lot better than he is anyway.

HOW AND WHEN TO TELL PEOPLE

While you may not have rushed to tell people in the first few days, circumstances are probably going to start requiring that you tell people around now and in the near future. Faxing a press release titled "Dumped and Heartbroken" to everyone you know is clearly unnecessary, but it is important for you, at a gentle pace, to start letting people know. The best way to handle telling people (except close friends and family whom you should call and tell within a few weeks of the breakup if you haven't already) is as it comes up.

When handling invitations that were intended for both of you, do not pretend that he is out of town or in the hospital. If you can't bring yourself to say it right now, just decline. But the next time mention that you are broken up. When people ask you how he is or what you two are doing this weekend, again, unless you are talking to someone you don't want to get upset around and don't feel you can keep it together, tell the truth. You want people to stop calling to invite the two of you to things or asking you about him, because it is upsetting, so why not sooner rather than later? You can just say, "We broke up." It's that simple. Don't expect it to make you feel great, but it's necessary.

When you have been going out for some time and have a lot of mutual friends, things can get a little hairy. I recommend that you lay low with the mutual friends and lean on friends who are truly yours, who came into this relationship on your team and are going to leave it with you. You will, of course, start hearing from mutual friends, friends you've made as a couple. Deal with them similarly to how you have dealt with others. If they don't already know, tell them when they ask about him or invite you two to do something. Try to avoid discussing it with them at length until you are feeling a little stronger.

HOW TO NEGOTIATE PEOPLE'S REACTIONS

Most people are cool when you let them know that you and your ex have broken up. Generally they say they are sorry and hope you feel better or something. Even though it's trite, if they don't know you that well, this response is appropriate.

Oftentimes, however, people will ask you what happened. Before you launch into it, consider if it makes sense to get into with them. If it's a friend or a colleague or family member who is a proven good friend, by all means tell him or her if you feel like it. But some people are just gossips and inappropriately nosy. You want to avoid, if you can, baring your soul to these kind of people. Also, beware of people who thrive on misery. I call them "drama zeligs." They don't care about you at all. It just makes them feel important to somehow be central to any kind of sorrow. And it's people like this who may take to calling you inappropriately to see how you are doing or may mention the breakup at an awkward time like a business meeting. Sometimes they are not even very good at pretending to care about you. They will use everything you say as a springboard to talk about their own experiences. You do not need someone you barely know crying on your shoulder right now.

And then there are people—you know who they are—who will take the news too gleefully or will somehow blame you. Again, you probably want to let these people know at some point that you and so-and-so are history, but don't feel under any pressure—and don't let them pressure you—into sharing more about what happened or how you are feeling than you want to. It's your breakup, and you don't have to talk about it with anyone you don't want to. With most people except those closest to you, you are totally within your rights to say you'd rather not talk about it, and even with them you are more than welcome to put off discussing anything until you feel ready to do so.

HIS FAMILY AND YOU

If you are like many of the women I know, you are actually a little relieved that you won't have to deal with your ex's family ever again. Things are simple. His family isn't reaching out to you, and it wouldn't occur to you to call them except for a fantasy in which you call them and tell them that they raised a total jerk.

However, it sometimes happens that you love your ex's family as much as—or even more than—you loved him. And sometimes your ex's family likes you better than your ex. Who knows? You may have even been pulled aside by his mother and told you were too good for her son. (So true.)

Ultimately, whether you were close to your ex's family, whether they think you are the greatest, whether you became good friends with his mother, or whether you can't stand them, I strongly recommend that you do not maintain contact with any members of his family. The only exception to this rule is if a member of his family was a friend of yours before you and your ex got together. Or, in the case of my friend Holly, when his family *is* your family. Yes, Holly dated her father's third wife's son. They even moved in together. Then he dumped her, and let's just say you wouldn't have wanted to be at their house for the holidays that year.

If members of your ex's family are reaching out to you—even if they are supportive of you and really nice—you should let them know that you appreciate their kindness and that you will miss them, but that you are going to need some time to figure things out and you'll be in touch when you are ready. When I say "when you are ready," in almost every case I mean never. As for you, I strongly recommend that you don't reach out to his family. Even if they think you are the best thing that almost happened to their son, it's too awkward. If they're planning to "talk a little sense into him" and suggest giving it a little time, thank them but say that you want to respect his decision. The truth is that even if members of his family tell you that your ex is an unworthy jerk, it's not going to make you feel better. You and I both know—however infuriating it is—that they are still related to him and love him, and that he, unlike you, will be in their lives forever.

You also have to think about your motivations here. Sure,

your ex's father is the most brilliant, funny this or that you've ever met, but do you really want to be in touch with him, or is this an indirect way of staying in touch with your ex and staying in his life? Lucy stayed friends with the sister of her ex for a decade after she and her ex broke up. For an entire ten years Lucy was a better, more thoughtful friend to the sister than the sister was to Lucy. Finally, Lucy realized that she'd always made more of an effort in their friendship because initially Lucy had been using the relationship as a way to stay connected to her ex. One day she woke up and realized that she hadn't cared about her ex in years, so why should she put up with his lame sister? They are no longer friends and Lucy feels that a weight has been lifted.

This is my bottom line: You have your own friends and family, and at some point, if you want, you are going to have a new man's family to contend with, so let your ex's family go and gently have them let you go too.

ANGER

Anger is an essential part of dealing with a breakup. It's an important part of accepting any loss in life. As women (which you may know or have heard on *Oprah*), it's often something that we are not very good at. We've been taught that it's unladylike, unbecoming, not nice, and that people, particularly men, won't like us if we express it. The list of reasons we've been socialized to contain our anger goes on and on, and it's truly unfortunate. Because around a breakup, as around many difficult passages in life, it's appropriate and healthy to be angry and to express it. If you don't, you may turn that anger inward, which is bad for you on every level. It's bad for your mental health and your physical health.

So there are two keys things to do: (1) allow yourself to be angry, and (2) do it in a way that doesn't do any lasting damage or land you in prison.

Allowing Yourself to Be Angry

You are probably not going to feel angry for a little while, and probably not in the first few days or even weeks of the breakup. In my experience, that's normal. You will be too hurt and depressed and then may spend some time blaming yourself, or drumming up sympathy for your ex in some way because he has problems too. If you find yourself getting angry soon, more power to you. If you don't, that's fine too. But you won't be able to really heal unless you get angry at some point.

If you find yourself sliding through the first month with only sadness and self-recrimination, it may be useful to ask a friend to help you get angry. Obviously, you want to ask someone who is not going to make you feel like an idiot for ever loving your ex. That will only make you feel worse. Pick someone who is sensitive to your feelings but a straight shooter and ask him or her to tell you why you should be angry at your ex. Several of your friends are probably angry at your ex right now because he has hurt you, and some of them may have never held him in high esteem. If they are protective of you, they will probably be able to recall for you every time he let you down and every hurtful thing he ever said. They will also be able to remind you how good and loving you were, how you were the best thing that ever happened to him, etc.

Keep in mind that even if your ex was a prince among men, it is totally legitimate for you to feel angry at him. Anyone who hurts you deeply should become the target of some angry feelings if you love yourself. That is a sign of healthy self-esteem, of you coming back to being you. It's a flag up if you can't get mad and, if so, you should seek therapy. Also, remember that anger and violence turned on yourself are NOT OKAY. If you are putting your fist through windowpanes or thinking a lot about doing things like that, you should seek help now.

No Jail Time

Of course, when you do get really angry, it may cross your mind to do some stupid, even criminal things. Evil thoughts are fine. Acting them out is not. You don't want your future compromised because some jackass broke up with you. So here are a few suggestions that won't land you in the slammer.

✿ Hannah likes to destroy crockery. When she gets mad, she drives to Costco and buys dozens of plates. She takes them home and then tosses them around, drops them on the floor, you get the drift. Personally, this takes more planning than I'm usually capable of, but maybe it will work for you. Just be sure to stay clear of flying shards of porcelain, and remember that even a small plate can make a big mess.

✿ Samantha is more creative. She makes voodoo dolls, some more elaborate than others, depending on how she's feeling. Then, as you would expect, she sticks pins in them. Usually she ends up burning them. I'm a touch superstitious so I couldn't bring myself to do it, and, as Samantha pointed out, I'm not handy with sewing and the like.

✿ Holly took up boxing to help her release some anger at her ex and spent hours at the gym for weeks with gloves on hitting a heavy sack hanging from the ceiling. I haven't tried this one, but it sounds really cool to me. It seems that women never get the opportunity to hit anything, and while hitting people isn't good, hitting something can be very therapeutic. However, I wouldn't try karate chopping wood blocks until you've had some instruction.

✿ Lucy, who is not much of a housekeeper, likes to clean when she is pissed. She will do the toilet, under the kitchen sink, inside the refrigerator, even closets. While this seems a little masochistic to me, it has the added benefit, once you are no longer feeling ballistic, that your house is totally clean.

✿ Emily goes running. Not running as in exercise. She literally runs and runs and runs until she basically drops. She injured one of her big toenails like this, and it was repulsive, but she didn't care and seemed to feel better. Again, this one is not for me but may help you.

✿ You've probably cried a lot already, but a really good cry with some screaming can help you release a lot of bad feelings and can be almost as exhausting as Emily's marathon. If you need help getting started, see "Top 5 Movies to Get the Tears Flowing."

✿ My cousin Annie finds destroying or defacing objects that belonged to her former beloved to be helpful. She likes to cut up a sweater or rip up letters or break a few of his records. This might annoy your ex if he eventually wants his stuff back but, in general, it's pretty harmless and helps Annie express some anger. This can, of course, get out of hand. Holly's sister went over to her ex's house when he was out and told his unsuspecting roommate that they were meeting and she was just going to chill out in his room. She then proceeded to demolish four lipsticks writing and drawing on the walls and mirrors. That was uncool. Her ex-boyfriend did call the police and she had to pay for damages. Then there is Lisa "Left-Eye" Lopez from TLC who decided to express anger at her boyfriend, Andre Rison, by burning his house to the ground. Needless to say this was not good and, if she hadn't had the cash to throw at a team of lawyers, could easily have landed her in the joint.

✿   I, personally, am a thrower. This can result in damage to objects you will later miss and will eventually involve cleanup. Maybe it's the years I spent playing softball, but I find hurling something of a medium weight as far and hard as I can to be a good feeling. Sometimes, however, in your anger, you can misjudge the weight of an object, with unfortunate consequences. This occurred to me one night when I grabbed a lamp (also stupid for electrical reasons) made of cinder block. I didn't expect it to be so heavy and, as a result, got almost no windup. Needless to say, the lamp landed only a foot in front of me and made a very costly dent in the floor.

These examples are not to say that you have to do anything physical or violent to release anger. But if you're going to, do it smart.

If all else fails, you may want to check out *Fuhgeddaboutit: How to Badda Boom, Badda Bing, And Find Your Inner Mobster* by Jon Macks. See suggested uses for toothpicks.

Expressing Anger to Him

While as a general rule I am against contacting him, it seems to me that the only really semiokay time to contact him is when you no longer care what he says or thinks. Sometimes this coincides with when you are furious. Oftentimes, however, anger sets in when you are still too vulnerable to have contact with him at all. Here are a few thoughts to consider (and remember, be honest with yourself).

A Final F—k Off

If you feel like you must tell him to go fly himself a kite permanently, maybe it isn't the worst thing you could do. But keep in mind that you only very recently broke up. Are you really capable of calling him and telling him that he's a jerk, that he sucks, that he's a fool, that you faked everything, and either not giving him time to respond or not caring what he says? Probably not. You don't want to leave yourself open to either being more hurt or to feeling so embarrassed that you end up wanting to apologize.

Also keep in mind that, except in the movies, it has *never ever* happened that being angry at a man has made him kinder, or made him realize that in fact he is madly in love with you and screwed up and is sorry, especially just after he's broken up with you. Most likely he'll be defensive and quite possibly nasty. So if that's going to upset you, and very likely it will, don't do it.

The point is that when you are mad, you need to be mad and do something that helps you express your anger but doesn't make you feel worse or ruin the rest of your life.

THE ROLE OF REBOUNDS

Reasonable friends of mine seem to have different opinions on this one, but one thing we all agree on is always be careful to make safety your first priority. Your judgment may not be as razor-sharp as usual.

When Holly has had her heart good and trounced, she is totally uninterested in men for a couple of months. She's never gotten back on the proverbial horse quickly. She's always preferred to let her grieving run its course until she feels a bit better. She says it hasn't felt like a matter of choice. Holly says that

the idea of dealing with someone new—even someone potentially great—when she's still in love with her ex just makes her
feel sick. She doesn't think she would be able to fake her way
through a date. And naturally, after a while, like her interest in
food, her interest in men and romance returns. It has never
taken so long that she or anyone else has gotten worried.

Holly suggests that the best thing that you can do for yourself after a breakup is to avoid dating for a month unless someone just knocks your socks off. If you preemptively decide that
you are taking a little time off from dating, then you don't have
to worry about whom you are meeting or not meeting. Holly
believes that if you call a time-out, no matter how much pressure you feel to meet someone, and no matter how old you are,
a month or so is not going to make a bit of difference.

Samantha disagrees. Her feeling is that you need to get back
out there and start dating immediately. Samantha suggests that
part of the recovery is meeting new people. She feels that
knowing that men are still interested in you helps a lot. And
because you are a little impervious to really being hurt—you're
already too hurt—it's a good time to date because you approach
men with more distance. They are not your ex so there is a
limit, at least for a while, to how much you care whether they
like you or not.

One week after Samantha's boyfriend broke up with her,
through her tears, she joined an on-line dating service. She
found a guy who seemed interesting to her, and she E-mailed
him. A week later they went out on a date. They ended up
going on three dates and he turned out to be a jerk, but Samantha didn't really care. She wasn't that attracted to him anyway.
But she did say that she felt it was good to know that there were
still lots of men out there and new ways to meet them if, in the

future, she felt as if she wasn't meeting anyone interesting through friends.

I feel that it's really up to you how you want to proceed with immediate redating and potential rebound relationships. If you feel that you aren't up to it, wait a few months, call a time-out. There is a lot of value in taking some time with yourself and your life and making it the best it can be. Quite possibly, this time spent recuperating can lead to better future relationships because the better you feel about yourself, the more attractive you are.

On the other hand, if you will feel anxious until you get back to dating, get back to dating as soon as you like. Just remember that it is unlikely that you are going to be able to feel much for the new guy, as you probably still have so much feeling for your ex. So even if you start dating new people right away, try to keep the focus on yourself. Dating shouldn't be used as a way to distract yourself from grieving or making changes in your own life or treating yourself righteously.

part two: TAKING CARE OF YOURSELF: YOUR BODY, YOUR HOME, YOUR SOUL

Obviously, when someone you love leaves you, your self-esteem takes a pretty serious blow. Now that you have gotten through the first few days, it's time to start doing a lot of big and small things to fight your way back to feeling good about yourself. How you deal with this month and the next few months is going to put you back on the happiness map and also make you ready to love someone new and let him love you, if you do it right.

The basic gist of getting through the first few days is to let yourself go and pass time until you don't feel as if your life is over. The "first month after the first few days" is a transitional period between total devastation and coming back to life. It is never my intention to make you feel worse about yourself or guilty about not doing something in this section, or in the two chapters that follow. It is important to keep in mind that throughout this period of loss you should be very forgiving of yourself. If at any point you fall off the recovery wagon, don't worry about it and just get back on board.

That said, the complete wallowing has got to come to an end sometime, and sometime during this month is a good time. Sure, you may find yourself relapsing into the fetal position from time to time and that's okay but it's no longer okay as a way of life. This section is going to require that you make a commitment to yourself to do some of the things that I recommend, the more the better. It may seem hard at first. You may still feel a little raw. But there is only one way to feel better, and that is to take yourself by the hand and get cracking.

PAMPERING

Even if you don't feel very motivated, you need to start pampering yourself. It takes a little energy, but it's good for you. Many of you may have gotten out of the habit of treating yourself well. Maybe it was all you could do to hold down your life and try to keep the relationship afloat. Or maybe, like too many women, taking good care of yourself has never been your strong suit. You're too busy, too broke, too generous with your time and energy. But there are no good excuses for not taking great care of the person who deserves it the most: you. Remember, there are a lot of things you can do for yourself, even if you are on a tight budget or don't have much free time. And if you have a lot of stress in your life besides this breakup, you really need to do them. Each time you do one of these, jump back and kiss yourself.

Your Space

Preparing to Pamper

In my experience, in order to properly pamper yourself, you must first do a little preparation, particularly in the space department.

Clean Up

Oftentimes, your space—your room, your apartment, your house—reflects the chaos that you are feeling. That's totally normal, but it's going to make it harder for you to feel that you can relax. So, like it or not, you are going to have to do something about it. If it seems overwhelming to clean up and organize things, do it in pieces, such as one room a day, or ask a friend to come over to help you or just keep you company and help you to motivate. You don't have to reorganize everything in your entire home now (and you may not want to ever), but it has to be tidy enough that it doesn't make you feel lousier than you already do. In anger or just because you are a neat person, you may have already given your place a great once-over. But if you haven't and can't bring yourself to do it, there are few things more luxurious than having someone else clean your home from top to bottom. Unless you live in a palace, this can be done for a reasonable amount of cash, and when you walk into your place after it's been cleaned, you will feel psyched despite yourself. Just be sure to get a referral from someone you trust.

Also, it's time to drop off that bundle of clothes that has been waiting to go to the cleaners or the tailors, or to drop off the shoes at the shoe repair place, or to put the CDs back in their cases. If you can't do it all at once, that's fine. Make a list and do one uncluttering thing a day.

Stock Up

As Hannah suggests, it is also hard to feel comfortable when you keep realizing that you don't have any food or other necessities in the house. Drag yourself over to the supermarket and stock up. Be a little extravagant. Fresh fruits and vegetables are a good call. Be sure also to get all the tampons, soap, laundry detergent, milk, coffee, and other staples that you will need to make you feel plentiful for at least a few weeks. And if you really want to live large, have it all delivered so you don't have much heavy lifting to do. Hannah says that doing this makes her feel responsible and cozy, and also makes sure that she has a lot of options to keep her eating habits pretty healthy even when she's feeling a little out of control.

Temperature Control

This sounds crazy, but a friend of mine lived in her apartment for six years before she finally did something about the fact that she was always cold. Her boyfriend left her and she slowly started taking better care of herself and got herself some space heaters and stopped wearing a hat and mittens indoors. If your space is chilly, go out and get some heaters. If it's always too hot, go out and get an air conditioner. These are good investments that will improve the quality of your life every minute of every day. There is no excuse for neglecting yourself this way.

Lighting

Living in a space that has unfortunate lighting can be a disaster and can lead you to pick at your face every five minutes which, as we all know, is not good. It may be as simple as getting some different bulbs, maybe they need to be softer, maybe brighter. A simple change in wattage can have a profound effect. Also, you may simply need to pick up one or two lamps, which honestly, if you shop carefully, can be reasonable. Emily swears that a $6 strand of clear white Christmas lights does wonders for the soul when properly hung.

Your Bathroom

I do a lot of my best grieving and healing in the bathroom because I am a bath addict. That means that in order to make the best use of this sanctuary, it cannot be a wreck. Most likely your bathroom is not huge, so you should be able to tackle this one fairly quickly, though it may require you to pick up a few items. You may need a hamper or some hooks or a little table for a book by your bath. You may want to get one of those rubber pillows for the bath or a no-slip bathmat or little carpet. You need to feel comfortable and cozy in this room even if you are just taking a hot shower every now and then.

If You've Been Living Together

In order to relax and lavish attention on yourself in a space that you and your ex used to share, you are probably going to need to do a little extra work. Obviously his stuff needs to go, if only out of sight for now. You also may want to reorganize the place so it feels a little different, or more like you. Ask a friend or neighbor to help you move around a few big pieces of furniture. It's fairly easy and can make a dramatic difference. Also, you may now notice that your life is quieter. There's only you and your movements making any noise. This may unsettle you a little at first. You may want to get some wind chimes (not effective in an apartment with no breeze) or one of those noise-making machines that offer crickets chirping or running water. Then there are the obvious noisemakers like a radio and the TV.

Flowers

Unless you have cats that are going to eat your flowers and throw up on your furniture, you must put down this book and go get yourself some flowers. If you don't have a vase or some reasonable substitute, get one. Put the flowers someplace central. It doesn't matter if the flowers are a handful of daisies or an elaborate arrangement of roses, just do it. This is no time to be stingy with yourself.

Sheets/Bedding

Right off the bat, if your sheets smell like your ex, wash them or, better still, take them to the laundry immediately. You might even consider new sheets—preferably in a high-thread count or in satin—especially when you may be spending a little extra time on your bed sobbing. If you and your ex spent a bunch of time on your bed, it may be additionally beneficial to change it a bit and make it just yours again. I have it on good authority from a sheet-obsessed friend that while sheets can be really expensive, you can still get some really suave ones at a reasonable price. Just because they are not the Pratesi sheets featured in every celebrity's bedroom in *InStyle* doesn't mean they won't do the trick. Other bed-related items can also help make you feel good. An extra pillow can be bought on a budget and make you feel truly decadent just reading in bed. And if you've been chilly at night, go straight out and get yourself a fluffy duvet.

Feng Shui/ Decluttering

Feng shui means organizing your home to maximize the flow of healthy *chi* or positive energy. It's an ancient Chinese practice that has recently gotten popular in some circles. There is a lot of information on-line, and most bookstores or libraries have books about it. Or you can get a really expensive feng shui consultant to come over and tell you where to put your stuff. You may also want to explore the more Western techniques of decluttering. Reorganizing your stuff and possibly getting rid of some of it can have far-reaching emotional impact. You may not be able to afford an organizing consultant, but flipping through the For Closets Only catalogue might give you some good ideas.

Tea

Holly, who is English, is, as you might expect, a bit of a tea fanatic. But she swears that going to a place that has lots of different teas and smelling them and then bringing them home and creating a pretty "display"of teas is a real pick-me-up. She recommends checking which are caffeinated and which aren't, and has a soft spot for green tea (which I know is good for you but is my least favorite) and jasmine (which smells great and tastes good too).

Your Body
Massage

In most places, you can get at least a half-hour massage for $75, maybe even a full hour. Do it if you can and go somewhere

where they also have a hot tub and a steam room and a sauna in the women's area. Get one of your friends to go with you so you can hang out together when you're not getting rubbed down.

If you can't afford to go anywhere, you can easily transform your bathroom into a steam room. Just close the door and run a really hot shower. Find a comfortable place to sit or make one for yourself, and breathe deeply. This particular tip is not recommended for those of you in areas facing drought.

Facials/Scalp Treatments/Sea, Herbal, and Mud Wraps/ Exfoliating

Like a massage, these are all soothing and make you feel like a princess, unless you overdo the exfoliating, in which case you will look like a cooked lobster and feel as if you've been skinned alive. Personally, I prefer to be covered in warm mud than have my face picked at when I'm feeling low, but any of the above are good. Some places also offer aromatherapy, which means that during your procedure they use oils and creams that smell nice. It's only a little bit extra and you deserve it.

If you can't afford to go to a salon, it's easy to do a mask or treatment for your hair at home. Any drugstore should have an ample selection of both, but you probably have some good items in your refrigerator. Plain yogurt or egg whites are good for your face. Just slather them on and leave them on for fifteen minutes and rinse off. You can also steam your face first by boiling water in a big pot and putting your head over the pot with a towel over your head. Annie suggests putting camomile tea in the pot or some rose petals, but just be sure not to burn yourself. You may want to test this procedure on your hand first. Another friend puts olive oil on her hair once a month. I was skeptical, but I poured some on my dry fly-away locks and slept on a towel with it in my hair. In the morning, my hair was a new woman, soft and shiny, so I guarantee this works. Finally, we have all heard that beer is good for hair, though you may not want to waste one. If you do any at-home treatments, make the experience special—light candles, put on soothing music, dim the lights.

Eyes

They say the eyes have it, and indeed the eyes do have several treats designed just for them. Emily recommends lavender scented eye-pillows. I have on several occasions taken advantage of the soothing powers of gel-filled eye masks. You look a little like Cat Woman *and* you feel good. In a pinch, a warm wet washcloth, a Ziploc with ice cubes in it, or cucumber slices will do. Hannah claims that similar gel-filled soothing pads are available for your neck, so if that's where you store your stress, get one now.

Naps

You may remember that as a child you took naps. Or you may have heard of the customary siesta in hot climates. My point is that naps are back and better than ever. The medical community has decreed that people who take short naps (around half an hour) have more energy, get sick less, and are in almost every way better than the rest of us. You just have to get your mind around this: Even if you don't notice the benefits, naps are good for you and are not a sign of laziness if kept to a reasonable nap a day. So take a nap when you feel a little tired or even when you don't. And if you can' t fall asleep, as I often can't, you still get almost all the benefits of napping if you just lie down, relax, and space out. Of course, the timing of your naps is important. For example, napping at work is probably a bad thing. Obviously, napping seven times a day is a pretty strong signal that you may be clinically depressed, and napping seven times a day while you are at work cries out narcolepsy and you should see your doctor.

Baths

There is literally no crisis I could have lived through without taking baths—the heat, the sound of running water, the fragrance of bubble bath. I highly recommend that you take a few baths ASAP. Bring in a cup of tea, bath oil or bath salts, some magazines, a book, some comics, some candles, rose petals, a radio tuned to a jazz station. If you don't have anything to put in your bath, go and check out all the different and delicious-smelling products at the drugstore and pick one that makes you smile. If you feel that taking a bath will take too much time or muss your hairdo, take a footbath. Throw some baby oil in there to smooth up your pedal extremities and relax. But be careful not to slip and crack your head open.

Manicures and Pedicures

Maybe you get them regularly so it's not that much of a treat, but if you're like me and you average a manicure every eighteen months, now is the time. Pedicures can be even more luxurious because your feet never get a break. You may even want to go to the drugstore on your way and pick up some fancy polish in a new color. Do not be self-conscious about crying at the salon. The ladies in there have seen a lot and definitely have an ample supply of Kleenex on hand.

Hair

It may be a good time to get a trim or some highlights or lowlights. I don't recommend that you do anything drastic in this first month (there will be time for that later), but why not freshen your hair up a bit? Myself, I don't really care how my hair looks, but I really like having someone else wash it and blow it out. In fact, if you don't want to make any changes to your hair or can't afford it, it's pretty reasonable to get it washed and blown. It feels really good and invariably looks better than when you do it at home.

Your Soul

Breakup Journal

Go out and buy yourself a notebook. It doesn't have to be anything fancy, a spiral notebook will do. You may actually want to burn this notebook eventually in some cleansing ritual, so I wouldn't break the bank here. Use this notebook to chronicle your breakup, your thoughts and feelings around it, and anything else you want to say. This notebook is totally private. Avoid being self-critical. This isn't a creative writing exercise. In fact, it doesn't matter what you write at all. But it does matter that you write. At first this may seem like a real drag, but I promise that it will help you defog and vent a lot of hurt and anger that is weighing you down.

Self-Help

You are reading this book. I hope it's helping you. Either way, there is a lot of helpful reading material out there, even if it's not directly related to breaking up, and you should check it out. Go to the largest bookstore near you and make an afternoon of it. Sit yourself down at a nice table at Barnes & Noble with a latte and bring every book off the self-help shelf with you. Bring a notebook. Write down anything that seems helpful. If you can afford it and something moves you, buy it and read it in your bath. The only upside to going through a crisis and feeling vulnerable is that you may find yourself open to new ways of living and making your life better than you would normally. Go with it.

Retail Therapy

This is no time to go into crazy credit card debt; actually, no time is a good time for that. But a few modest purchases may make you feel empowered without making you so anxious about your finances that you want to throw up. As Samantha points out, unless you are in a midlife crisis, you don't need a Porsche to feel better. And you don't want to buy a really expensive alligator coat or cashmere bikini because you are feeling desperate and then be unable to return it when you come back to your senses. Stick to items that will make you feel playful and attractive but aren't too pricey. Samantha recommends any kind of cosmetics, especially lipstick, hair bands, or cute barrettes, sassy bras and underwear, a new nightgown, or slippers. She also suggests that you can find cool jewelry at a reasonable price and that a really big ring can make you feel like you kick ass again. Another reason to stick to accessories is that unless you love how your body looks in a changing room, you don't want to get involved with any body-image issues right now. If you are going to shop for clothes, beware of the lighting in the changing room at Bloomingdale's, which could reduce even Elle MacPherson to tears.

Shoes, of course, are an entirely different matter. Again,

while you don't want to do anything financially insane right now, you may very well need to buy some low-to-medium priced shoes. In my estimation, there are two kinds of women: women like me who are empowered by clunky platforms and women like Lucy who find that a stiletto-heeled strappy number makes them invincible. Either way, there are a lot of shoe stores these days that do impressive knockoffs of the latest from Blahnik and Kelian, and you should investigate them posthaste. Even if it's snowing outside, you can still get a rush from wearing your new kicks in your pad.

The World of Alternative Healing

In recent years, Eastern healing arts have taken the U.S. of A. by storm. It may not all be your personal trip, or available where you live, but you may want to check out some of the following: chakra therapy, Reiki, reflexology, acupuncture, acupressure, nia, vipassana meditation. You should look into any new "treatments" carefully, but it seems that you can't lose when you try some new method of healing. On the other hand, if you are afraid of needles, acupuncture would probably be more traumatic than soothing.

Incense, Candles, and Oil Burners

You may have forgotten about incense. I almost did until I saw some at the farmers' market down the road and remembered how much some of those fragrances repulsed me. I also remembered how much I liked some of them and realized that there is no scent these days that doesn't exist in incense form. Candles are great and, it seems, the whole country is hip to them—scented ones are even available at Rite Aid. Get some and light them. They are pretty, and some of them smell terrific. Just remember to put them out. Also, burning sage or eucalyptus smells delicious and is said to ward off evil spirits. Or you may find that sticking to oil burners is the neatest and least hazardous way to go. Like incense, there are oils available in almost every scent.

Music

Josie says that when she was with her ex, she stopped listening to music. It may be time to dig into your collection and pull out some of your favorite music—music that's really yours and doesn't have any associations with your ex. Josie's father is a concert cellist and she has an extensive classical music collection to dip into, but whatever makes you feel good will do the job. It also may be time to take yourself to the record store and get a new CD you've been wanting or replace a lost favorite.

Go to the Sun

On the off chance that you have lots of vacation time saved up or you are a woman of leisure and have some cash lying around, you might want to take a vacation somewhere warm. I've never been able to just jet off like this or even sneak away to visit my great-aunt Marvelle in Boca for a few days, but I've dreamed of it. Even though I like skiing, going to a place where the climate is harsh doesn't seem appealing when life itself seems harsh enough. But a little sun, with full-body SPF coverage, can work wonders on a bruised soul. It's probably best to take a friend with you or go someplace where you have a friend in case you are still feeling a little shaky.

If you decide to take a trip or if you have to travel for work or, God forbid, you have to go to your best friend's wedding across the country, always be sure to pack a "safety kit." This kit should be fairly compact but include some of the things you will need to feel comforted and sane if you start freaking out. You may want to include an eye pillow, your favorite CD, a book of poems, your stuffed bunny rabbit. If you start feeling horrible, take a few minutes out and get with your safety kit. It will make you feel better. Also, imagine yourself in the "safe place" you created earlier.

Cooking

This may sound more like torture than pampering, and if that's how you feel, you should skip it. On the other hand, you may want to give it a shot because, even though it may seem unlikely, cooking can often lift your spirits when they are low, especially when you are not cooking under pressure, as when your ex's parents were coming over for dinner.

The first great thing about cooking is that it is distracting. You have to pay some attention to what you are doing but, here, you aren't too concerned about the result so you won't be stressed out. The second good thing about cooking is that even if you are just making pancakes, it feels really productive and you get to see the fruits of your labor pretty quickly. Another thing is that if you choose to make something you like or something healthy, it can also make you feel as if you are taking good care of yourself. Alternately, if you decided to make something for someone else, you will make him or her happy and that will make you feel good.

Hannah recommends soup because you can keep it around and eat it over several days and it will make you feel as if you have something delicious in your house. And if you make soup involving vegetables, it can be therapeutic to cut them up. Lucy prefers to make bread. She enjoys the kneading process and likes that a loaf of bread makes a nice and easy gift to almost anybody.

Arts and Crafts, Etc.

These suggestions may not seem like pampering, but little projects can be very soothing and distracting. You may not think of yourself as a talented artist, but that is totally irrelevant here. Paint a landscape with watercolors. Paint your bathroom a new color. Draw your pet. Make a mix tape. Make Easter eggs. Make a collage of photos of your friends. Make a collage of pictures from magazines that you like. Make a collage of your "safe place." Knit if you know how to. Learn how to if you can handle it. Glue some toothpicks together. Make a card for someone. Dye a faded T-shirt a new color. You may end up creating something you will want to keep forever. You may not. It doesn't matter. The activity is more important than the result.

CONCLUSION

If you have made it through the first month, you deserve a big hug, and if I were at your house I'd do it myself. The first few days and the first month are the worst, and now they are behind you. Do something to congratulate yourself. Take a friend out to dinner. Buy yourself more flowers. Get some champagne. You may not feel as if you've done that much—you may still feel awful. But you have lived through this time and shown yourself some kindness, and that is plenty.

Yeah, there are still going to be some hard times ahead. You are probably going to have flashbacks when you will feel like you are reliving the initial pain of the breakup. And, of course, you are still grieving. But the general truth is that it's never going to be as bad as it was. There are still issues that relate to your ex and the relationship that are going to crop up, and I am going to address them. But the focus will center more on the most important person around: you. You've probably been on cruise control for a while. That's fine, but now it's time for you to get back in the driver's seat.

Top 5 Heartbreak Albums You Probably Don't Own

1. **Bonnie Raitt—***Streetlights*: She's known some hard times in the arena of love but lord knows she's made the most of them. This album is full of poignant gems like "That Song About the Midway."

2. **Nina Simone—***The Blues*: This is my favorite Nina Simone album, and it may be the most sensual album of all times. If songs could be bruises, then they'd sound like "Do I Move You?" and "In the Dark."

3. **Van Morrison—***Astral Weeks*: This album follows the arc of a love affair from beginning to end and is Van's most emotional album. At first you may wonder what happened to traditional song structure, but eventually listening to this album will feel as natural as breathing.

4. **Rickie Lee Jones—***Pirates*: I read on Amazon that this album is about Rickie Lee's failed relationship with mentor/lover Tom Waits. I can neither confirm nor deny this, but I will say that "We Belong Together" is one of the most beautiful and wrenching songs ever.

5. **Frank Sinatra—***In the Wee Small Hours*: Loneliness, thy name is Frank! They say that memories of Ava Gardner caused Frank to break down and weep (in a manly way, of

course) after he recorded "When Your Lover Has Gone." You may not think that Frank and you have a lot in common, but if you listen to this perfect album you will realize that you and the Chairman of the Board are actually soulmates.

Top 5 On-Line Sites to Amuse, Enlighten, and Beautify

1. **www.dailycandy.com**: This site is most handy if you live in Los Angeles, New York, or London, but there is still much to browse on it even if you don't. Definitely the place to find out what is chic right now.

2. **www.beautybuzz.com**: You can't buy products here, but you can get the scoop on them by people who aren't afraid of getting fired. I don't know who these people are, but Lucy says that the recommendations on this sight are right on, and she is a product maven. Check out the color descriptions—a real labor of love.

3. **www.bathdiva.com**: You can buy products on this site and it's awesome. The soaps make me salivate, and the rubber duckies with the cool shades are a slick addition to any bath.

4. **www.astro.com**: If you know the time, date, and place of your birth, this site will do your personal astrological chart for you, and can keep your information so that you can get a personal horoscope every day.

5. **www.spiritweb.org/spirit/feng-shui.html**: This is the feng shui part of this site, but the entire New Agey site is healingish related. This is a great way to waste a lot of time and learn some groovy things.

Top 5 Cartoon Books About Love, Women, Cats, and Shoes

1. ***101 Reasons Why a Cat Is Better Than a Man*** by Alia Zobel, illustrated by Nicole Hollander: Sure, you could probably just grab a pen and write this book yourself, but Zobel has already done it. Why not save yourself the time and get her book?

2. ***The New Yorker Book of True Love Cartoons*** by *The New Yorker*: It's funny that they named this collection "True Love." A better title might have been "True Love—Not!" You can't beat the range of drawings and perspectives. Also, this book is more coffee table friendly than *101 Reasons . . .*

3. ***Never Tell Your Mother This Dream*** by Nicole Hollander: Look, Nicole Hollander is a brilliant illustrator, but she is also a comic genius. Her character Sylvia is usually chain-smoking and drinking beer in the bath. This may be the funniest book of cartoons ever.

4. ***Love Is Hell*** by Matt Groening: His cartoons might look familiar to you, probably because he created the Simpsons. But this book is raunchier, darker, and more cynical than anything they could put on TV.

5. ***Only Love Can Break Your Heart, But a Shoe Sale Can Come Close:*** **A Cathy Collection** by Cathy Guisewite: I think Cathy can be a little cutesy, but she is a classic.

Top 5 Movies to Get the Tears Flowing

1. ***Beaches***: Best friends, jealousy, possible man stealing, fame, divorce, and terminal illness. There is nary a moment in this movie when you get a break from uncontrollable sobbing.

It's as if the people who make Kleenex produced this one just to move product.

2. *Terms of Endearment*: Best friends, mothers and daughters, and again terminal illness. It's impossible to conceive of an entire audience of people watching this movie in a theater without causing a flood.

3. *Philadelphia*: Love, discrimination, AIDS, Antonio Banderas's eyelashes. Even the coldest heart melts as Tom Hanks fights the system and death, and Bruce Springsteen's song "Streets of Philadelphia" provides the perfect sound track for dry heaving.

4. *The Joy Luck Club*: I saw this movie with my mother and we were almost asked to leave because we blew our noses too many times. It wasn't pretty and neither were we.

5. *A Walk on the Moon*: Talk about tugging at the heartstrings. Liev Schrieber is such a good man and a loving father, but Viggo Mortensen is so smoking hot. Diane Lane faces some hard choices in this flick and so will you if you don't bring your hankie (you'll be stuck between using your sleeve or the jacket of the person next to you).

Top 5 At-Home Remedies for Crying Eyes

1. **Metal Spoon**: This is as easy as grabbing two metal spoons, running them under some cold water for a minute, and resting the spoons facedown on your eyes. If you can't do this, then you've got problems far more serious than the heartbreak at hand.

2. **Hemorrhoid Cream**: This was news to me, but when I called Lucy, she said, "Yeah, all the beauty pageant contest-

ants do it." Josie, on the other hand, thought it sounded dangerous. The deal is that ingredients like shark's liver oil (sounds tasty) reduce swelling. So spread some on your eyelids and watch the puffiness disappear. I recommend doing it rather carefully and reading any possible warnings on the tube like "May Cause Blindness."

3. **Thin Cucumber Slices**: Cindy Crawford recommends this one and so do I, which is about all we have in common. But she never has puffy eyes so try it.

4. **Black Tea Bags**: Say you are fresh out of spoons, cucumbers, and hemorrhoid cream but you happen to have some black tea around. Just soak the tea bags in cold water for ten minutes and apply them to your eye area, pressing on them gently. Something in the tea drains retained water. I may tape fifty of them together and apply them to some other parts of my body.

5. **Raw Potato Slices**: Sure you've got puffy eyes from crying, but what about dark circles from crying all night long and getting no sleep? No worries. Just get a potato, slice it up, and apply the slices to your eye/undereye area. The potassium in the spuds is absorbed into your face and reduces unsightly darkness.

Top 5 Nail Polish Colors

1. **Revlon Red**: This is classic—feminine but full of attitude. I don't have much length in the nail department and if you don't either, rest assured because the lady who works at the gas station near my house promised me that short red is *the* in look. Also perfect for toes.

2. **Chanel Vamp**: Strike a pose, *chérie*. With nails "vamped" out in deep reddish-purple, which looks black in dim lighting, you are dangerous.

3. **OPI Japanese Rose Garden**: If pink is your thing, this is for you. The soft bubble gum creme has a come-hither-and-wither quality that you may want to affect these days. If you can't find it in stores, call 1-800-341-9999.

4. **Maybelline Ultimate Wear Chambray Blue**: This slightly opalescent blue with hints of gold may match the blue mood that you are in, but make no mistake, blue is bad-ass and also empowering on toes.

5. **Estée Lauder White Petal**: Maybe you don't want to say that much with your nails right now besides letting people know that your instinct to groom yourself magnificently is stronger than your desire to sob 24/7. In this case, a lightly opaque white creme will do the trick.

Top 5 Children's Books to Revisit

1. *Eloise* by Kay Thompson: This is the best book ever. Eloise is only six and she understands the importance of amusing oneself and of room service. Perhaps that's because she is basically an orphan living in a hotel, but no matter. I dare you to come up with a more genius way to pass the time than braiding your turtle's ears.

2. *Harriet the Spy* by Louise Fitzhugh: So Harriet is a little weird and it's not cool when her journal falls into the hands of her friends, but I've been eating tomato and mayonnaise sandwiches ever since I read this book more than twenty years ago. It also taught me early to keep my journal in a safe place—a very valuable lesson.

3. ***Pippi Longstocking*** by Astrid Ericsson Lindgren: Pippi rules! She dances with robbers and plays tag with the fuzz. Both activities are inadvisable, but you have to admire her joie de vivre.

4. ***Ramona the Brave*** by Beverly Cleary: Things may seem rough now, but can you remember what a drag it was starting school for the first time? Ramona brings it all back—the fear, the heartache, the courage, the crayons.

5. *A Little Princess* by Frances Hodgson Burnett: What a page turner! Poor Sara, a teeny, freezing, hungry little indentured servant, manages to keep herself together in the face of adversity and injustice, and carries the day because she knows being a princess is really about strength of character and kindness. Sara helps you get in touch with the little princess inside of you.

Top 5 Lipstick Colors

1. **Revlon Blackberry**: It's a little dark, but if you pat some of it off and toss on a little gloss or Chapstick, you will have the sexiest lips in town. You should be able to pick this up anywhere.

2. **Clinique Grapestain**: This was one of the greatest lip colors around and looked good on everybody. So why, you ask, did Clinique decide to discontinue it? The woman at the Macy's Clinique counter almost broke down in tears when I asked her for some because she said I was the hundredth or so person to ask her about it that day. If you'd like to try this splendid color, I invite you to join me in bombarding Clinique with calls asking them to bring it back. The number of their corporate headquarters is 212-572-3800.

3. **Mac Viva Glam I**: Not only is this a happening dark brick red and, according to the saleswoman at a MAC store in LA, it's "the prettiest red around," but 100 percent of the sales of the lipstick go to help people living with AIDS. MAC has its own stores, but you can also buy their products at www.MACcosmetics.com or call 1-800-387-6707 to order them.

4. **Benetint by Benefit**: It's a "lip and cheek stain." That may sound a little frightening but it looks fly and, best of all, Benetint smells like roses. It's purplish pink and you can get it at www.sephora.com.

5. **Vision Lip Lux by Vincent Longo**: This berryish gloss is so fabulous that I have basically stolen it from a friend of mine who left it at my house. It looks extrasnazzy when applied with a brush. You can also buy it at www.sephora.com.

Note: Obviously, you need a lip pencil to make your lips look really great. My girlfriends and I recommend Wet'n'Wild #666, Chanel Nude, Bobbie Brown Raisin, and MAC Plum.

QUIZ #3

What Have You Done for You Lately?

Not to be a hard-ass, but it's time to check in on whether you've been naughty or nice—to yourself. If it turns out that someone doesn't love you the way you wanted him to, you must lavish extra love and attention on yourself.

Does your apartment look like a tornado just hit it?

If the answer is NO: High five, baby. Maybe this doesn't cheer you up, but I guarantee that it would be a lot worse if you had to step over pizza boxes to get to the door.

If the answer is YES: Here is the deal: You MUST clean up or get help cleaning up ASAP. Either do it yourself or pick up the phone and get a friend to come over and help you or get a referral for a cleaning service. You cannot even start to cheer up unless your home is reasonably tidy. Feeling overwhelmed triggers sad feelings, and there are few things that make a person feel more overwhelmed than looking around her living space and not being able to find a place to sit.

Do you still have your ex's things all over your house?

If the answer is NO: Nice going. Keeping that stuff around is just not good.

If the answer is YES: Honey, what are you waiting for? This is about what is good for you, and it's just not good for you to cling to the past. If there are a few things you feel you must save, put them in a box in the back of closet. You have got to clear your heart out to make room for yourself and for the next guy, and the best place to start is clearing the old guy's useless stuff out of your apartment.

Does looking at yourself in the mirror frighten you?

If the answer is NO: I'm assuming you're back on track with hygiene and grooming, which is good for anyone close enough to smell you and good for your self-esteem.

If the answer is YES: Get in the shower *now*. Wash your hair and shave whatever parts you used to shave. Moisturize. Put on clean clothes. Dab on a little perfume. It's high time for you to get a grip on yourself. You cannot go on neglecting the basics and feeling that you look gross.

Are booze, diet soda, and junk food the only things in your fridge?

If the answer is NO: Perfume and eye cream and that kind of stuff don't count, so if you thought that would be all right, think again. If you've got food that has nutritional value, then you are on the right track. Just be sure to eat some of it.

If the answer is YES: Grab your wallet and your jacket and go to the grocery store. What are you thinking? You can't feel better emotionally—under these or any circumstances—unless you give your body some of the things it needs, like protein and vitamins. You may have forgotten that your body and your mind are connected, but they haven't.

Is there at least one CD in your collection that has been purchased in the last year?

If the answer is NO: You may be broke, but are you also being miserly with yourself? It would seem so. Music is essential. It's food for the soul, and one or two new (or used) CDs a year is not unreasonable even if you are hurting for cash. At the very least, have a friend make a copy of a CD you've been wanting. If the answer is YES: Rock on.

If you can't get it together to treat yourself decently by now, you either need to get cracking or you may want to call in some help. You have lost a man, but you should not have lost all regard for yourself. If you've been treating yourself well, you rule.

3. months two and three:
BABY-STEPPING BACK TO REALITY

part one: INSIDE YOUR HEAD

Just because I've said that the worst is over, you may not be feeling that way yet. You are probably no longer living in crisis mode, which is progress, but reality is sinking in and that can be very painful too. Also, you may not have the support that you once did. Friends and family may feel that enough time has passed that you should be healed by now, or they may act that way because they think that not talking about the relationship and your ex will help you move on faster. Also, you may be reluctant to talk about how you're feeling or the breakup because you are embarrassed that it's still on your mind so much of the time, and you feel self-conscious that you are not "over it." In addition, time is probably moving faster for your friends and family than it feels like it is for you. Here's the thing: It's totally normal to be thinking about your ex and the relationship and the breakup almost all the time. It means you are coming to terms with this loss. When someone who was constantly a part of your life suddenly drops out of your life, it's a little like a death and it's going to take a while for you to get used to. It's going to take your mind a lot of thinking and time to understand and to accept. True emotional healing is unfortunately not a speedy process.

The challenge of the next two months is to balance letting yourself grieve while not getting too stuck inside your head. You need to let yourself feel and think about what has happened, but you also need to slowly start reconnecting with the world as the incredible single woman that you are. I'm going to address some new issues that may be surfacing and get a little more in-depth on some issues that came up before.

LONELINESS

It's important to keep in mind that loneliness is an extremely common emotion. Everyone feels lonely sometimes. Single people, married people, teenagers, widowed people, pregnant women, grandparents, party animals—everyone. Loneliness can creep into one's heart as easily at a crowded disco or at home alone. It's not a good feeling, but it's not something to be ashamed of and it's not something to fear—it's part of being alive. One of the scariest things about being single again can be an overwhelming feeling of loneliness or feelings of a new kind of loneliness. These may be feelings that you are uncomfortable with and they may panic you.

Let's consider the different kinds of loneliness and see what feels relevant to you.

✿   Existential loneliness—big questions. Why are we here? Is there a God? What is the meaning of life? What happens after death? Am I totally insignificant? Coke or Pepsi? Almost everyone thinks about these questions at some point, but if you're already feeling lost and you start thinking about them, it can make you feel like a tiny little speck in a vast and mysterious universe and you can begin to feel mighty lonely.

✿   Social and community loneliness—where are *my* people? This is the loneliness of not feeling like you belong to a group. It is increasingly common as we often live far from family and childhood friends, and less in ways that make us feel part of communities. After all, humans are, like dogs, pack animals, and the feeling of having no pack can be lonely.

✿   Unexpected loneliness—different wavelengths. Often, in serious or long-term relationships of any kind, there can be a presumption of closeness. For example, if a person has known you since you were five, or knows your schedule and what kind of toothpaste you use and you two sleep in the same bed, you often assume that you are close. It can be very unpleasant to discover that familiarity and closeness are not necessarily the same thing, especially in an intimate moment or when you are trying to share an important thought. You feel unexpected loneliness when you realize that you and your sibling or boyfriend or parent are on completely different wavelengths. This kind of loneliness can be normal—people are not always in sync but can get back in sync—or it can be symptomatic of the beginning of a painful growing apart. You may have experienced this type of loneliness before your breakup even if things were going well between you and your ex.

✿ Experience-specific loneliness—I am ultimately experiencing this alone. There are many times—even when you are in a close relationship or connecting well with others—that you experience something unpleasant and no one can experience it quite the way you are, which can make you feel lonely. Here are two examples:

You are on the phone with your best friend and you and she are talking about the breakup. She is being so wonderful and understanding. God knows, she's been through many painful breakups herself. Suddenly, her toddler is screaming for her and she has to jump off the phone. You hang up and you feel lonely. You realize that as amazing as your best friend is, she's just not going through what you are going through right now.

Your parent (God forbid) passes away. Your spouse is incredibly supportive; he really does love your parent too. But it's clear that as great and upset as he is, he's just not going through what you are going through. He just doesn't know your parent the way you do; it's not his parent.

✿ Romantic loneliness—no life partner. Bells may be going off for you around this one right now. You are feeling the absence of someone to share your life with who will share his life with you. No matter how many close friends and colleagues and family members you have, nothing can make this kind of loneliness go away except for a close, intimate relationship.

You may be feeling one or several or all of these types of loneliness, and that's totally normal. You're in a vulnerable place and you are processing a major change and also, most important, you are simply human. Here are some things to keep in mind:

✿   Loneliness is made worse by worrying about it. It's similar to when you can't sleep and you start freaking out about everything you have to do the next day. You seize up and feel more panicked, but if you relax into the not-sleeping you are much more likely to actually be able to fall asleep. If you relax when you feel lonely, rather than tensing up with fear and anxiety about the future, you realize it's not pleasant but it's manageable.

✿   No matter what type or types of loneliness you've got going on and no matter how intense it feels, you need to remember that it will pass. Just as it is human to experience loneliness, it's also true that your average person's loneliness dissipates over time and that invariably circumstances change. Sure, you may feel some kind of loneliness sometimes, but you will not feel intense loneliness around the clock. Our systems just aren't built to sustain it.

✿   Not to needlessly make you think about painful experiences in your past, but consider this: You may feel that you've never felt as lonely as you do right now, but is that really true? How did you feel as a kid or teenager your first day at a new school or at a new sleep-away camp? Or how about some times in high school? Or how about sitting in your room as a kid and hearing your parents fight? But do you still feel the loneliness you did on these previous occasions? Most likely you don't. It came, hurt, and passed, as will any hard-core loneliness you are feeling now.

✿   Loneliness does not mean that no one loves you or no one cares for you. You probably have lots of people who care about you and who love you. They may not always be in sync with you or sharing exactly what you are going through, but your ex was not—and is not—the only person who shared in your life. No one man will ever be.

✿ You have some control over how lonely you are, now and always. You can still be connecting with people, even if it's not with the man of your dreams. The difference between feeling most types of loneliness and not being lonely isn't that you have a man in your life; the difference is *connecting* with people.

✿ Romantic loneliness is the kind of loneliness that you have the least control over, as we all know. But that doesn't make it any more worthwhile to freak out about. You probably experienced it before you met your ex and then you met him and you didn't feel it anymore. And that's just how it's going to be when you meet the next man whom you get close to—it'll just disappear. Fear of never meeting another man only makes romantic loneliness worse, and it doesn't get you anywhere except more miserable. So do your best to accept that this is how you are feeling now and don't feed its fire by letting it scare you as well.

✿ On a positive note, chances are excellent that your ex is feeling lonelier than you are. Women tend to have more connections in their lives than men, more close relationships, and it's quite possible that you were the closest person in your ex's life while you have several people in your life—friends, siblings—whom you are equally close to on an emotional level. (Do not, of course, use this thought as reason to start feeling sorry for your ex now.)

Note: If months go by and you still feel that you aren't able to connect with anyone, even people you used to, you may want to get yourself some help. You may be having a hard time feeling comfortable with yourself, which always creates problems connecting with other people. This is common around loss and can improve with professional help. Take this step because there is no reason that someone as amazing as you shouldn't be having a connected life—with or without a man.

HOME—AND ELSEWHERE—ALONE

Being alone can be great, but if it's new for you then it can take some getting used to. If you and your ex spent every evening together or lived together, you are probably going to be a little shaky with being alone for a while. It's still something of a shock to your system how much it seems as if your life has changed in such a short time.

It's quite common for people to forget that their ex is no longer a part of their lives and then catch themselves. If you have ever had someone close to you die, you may recognize some similarities. You think of something that you would like to say to your ex and then realize he's not around and isn't going to be. Or you see an ad for a movie your ex would like and think you two should go see it and then you remember that you aren't together anymore. It can really bring you low when this happens. It feels for a moment as if you are going through the loss again for the first time. These experiences suck, but remember that you've made it this far through worse and you will be okay. I 100 percent promise that gradually both the frequency of these kinds of thoughts and their impact on you will lessen. In the meantime, it's neither good nor appropriate to contact him to share your thoughts (see "The Slippery Slope: Being in Touch" section later in this chapter).

One strategy for being newly alone is to start small. Don't spend a lot of time alone; you simply don't have to. It doesn't make you a stronger or better person to push yourself harder than is comfortable for you on this front. In fact, it's downright mean of you.

Home

If being alone at your home for long stretches is initially uncomfortable—you feel sad, lost, aimless—don't spend an entire evening there without company for a while. Go to a friend's house, have a friend come over, go to your mom's, go to a class. You can get used to being alone at home over time. After Lucy's boyfriend moved out, Lucy decided that being home alone for more than three hours in the evenings was unbearable. For a few weeks, she limited her home alone time to three hours. Then she moved up to five-hour stretches. Then seven hours. Then she forgot about feeling weird being home alone and it became a nonissue. She felt comfortable being home alone again.

If you work at home, this is going to be trickier. I recommend that you make an effort to break things up for a while. (This may be a good idea anyway, because working at home can make anyone feel crazy.) Work for two hours, then take a walk around the block. Work for another hour, then meet a friend for coffee. Work some more and go to your neighbors' to watch a movie, or have them over.

Everywhere

I'm going to talk more about dealing with being single again "out and about" at the end of this chapter and in the next. What I'm referring to here by "everywhere" is the everyday outings that you may not have been doing alone before, like going to the Laundromat, grocery shopping, etc. It's also possible that you did a lot of these things alone before but now doing them alone makes you unexpectedly sad. So the same rules apply as with being home alone: Start small and ask a good friend, neighbor, or sibling to do some of these things with you. Make an afternoon of errands, buy your errandmate a snazzy latte at some point and then have him or her over for dinner. Who knows? Maybe your errandmate has a few mundane things to do that he or she would welcome your company for.

FANTASIES

It seems that everyone—once the crisis wears off a little and your friends stop calling every five minutes to see if you are all right—suddenly develops a rich fantasy life. If you feel as if you're going crazy because your thoughts are pretty out there, don't worry. You're not. I'm not saying that you aren't especially creative and original, but know that a lot of people have had a variation on your fantasy and things never got out of control. Usually, fantasies become less compelling over time, though no doubt there always will be one or two men in your past whom you hope to run into down the line when they are fat and bald and broke, and you are at your absolute best.

Here are a smattering of the most common fantasies that my friends and I have had. I have classified them by general theme. Do any of them sound familiar?

Despair

Let's start with these first because they are the grimmest and, obviously, least fun.

For a while after her breakup, Josie was haunted in her daydreams by visions of herself at something like seventy-five years old and obese with thin greasy hair wearing a dirty and tattered housedress in a dark cramped apartment reeking of cat feces. The phone never rings because she has no friends (they are all off with their perfect families living perfect lives in St. Bart's) and no children and no job. The cats *and* she eat cat food.

I hope, this seems a little off even if you're having similar thoughts. It's quite a stretch from the attractive and smart thirty-four-year-old Josie to her "fantasy Josie" as it is no doubt from you to your imagined you. There is no way your whole life's going in the crapper because of your ex.

Holly was traumatized by the prospect of walking down the street, not looking particularly good, and running into her ex with his new girlfriend (not that he had one in real life). The new girlfriend is a woman Holly knows—it's a friend of her ex's whom she always suspected had a crush on him and basically looks like Holly but better—a little slimmer, a little more self-assured, enviably dressed. Holly's ex seems happier than ever. He has a new kick-ass job and is holding his new woman's hand affectionately, which is not something that he was ever comfortable doing with Holly. In Holly's "nightmare," her ex has none of the issues that he had when they were going out; he even seems to be a bit taller and less bald than she remembers. Somehow, Holly can tell that her ex is having the close, committed, giving relationship with this woman that he and Holly never had. And then she notices the engagement ring on the new woman's hand, which is crushing because her ex had said that he didn't think he would ever get married. Holly walks away, alone and dejected, hearing her ex and his new woman sharing a laugh.

I think that every woman has had a version of this fantasy. The thing of it is that there is *no way* that your ex has become the person that you had hoped he would in the time since you two have broken up. In fact, he probably will never be the person you hoped he would be. Whatever problems he had before, he's still got, and whatever problems he had with you, he'll probably have with the next woman (not that there will be a next woman).

Revenge

Emily, who is not an actress nor to my knowledge has the slightest interest in acting, imagined herself into a superstar on a level with Jennifer Aniston. In fact, Emily and Jennifer were pretty tight in this scenario—cooling out at each other's pools, borrowing each other's clothes, giggling together on set. Anyway, one evening Jennifer and Emily are out on the town at some posh restaurant with Brad and Emily's boyfriend Mark McGrath (I think she'd been watching a lot of MTV) when the waiter shows up at their table and, lo and behold, it's Emily's ex. He's looking worse for wear. Since he left her, his life has become a disaster. He was fired from his job at Goldman Sachs, he's living at the YMCA, and his fair-weather friends are nowhere to be found. Emily, feeling pity for her ex, introduces him to everybody as an old friend and makes a note to herself to leave a nice tip. But the evening takes an unexpected turn when Tony Bennett shows up to serenade Emily, and Mark drops to his knees and pulls out a diamond as big as the Ritz. Emily is so consumed with joy that she doesn't even notice her ex run from the restaurant into the cold night air, truly a broken man (but because this is her fantasy, Emily has actually created this part too).

One classic revenge fantasy was brilliantly articulated by "tantric man" Sting in the song "Can't Stand Losing You." You may remember that he bids a final farewell to his indifferent ex and promises her that she'll be sorry when he's dead. I think when someone hurts you, it's an easy step to imagining him guilt-ridden, heartbroken, and sorry as can be at your funeral where everyone is saying the best things about you (all true, of course). The glaring problem with this fantasy is that for it to come true you have to be dead, which is obviously not worth it. It's really not good to think that a dramatic final gesture will affirm your closeness with your ex. Not to mention all the terrific people—excluding your ex—who would be devastated by your passing . . .

Reconciliation

I once had a boyfriend who was a musician and left to go back on tour. We went from being inseparable to him just never calling. I was, of course, devastated, because even though he was a musician (and maybe partly because of it) I was madly madly in love with him. Anyway, in the demented logic of my fantasy world, I would have to so attract his attention such that he would come back from the road and realize his mistake. It had to be fairly dramatic and perhaps involve someone he loved much more than me (which in hindsight could probably have been anyone). So it went like this: I would be innocently walking down the street and a madman would appear waving a gun in the air, shooting wildly. With catlike swiftness, I would jump in front of a bullet that was intended for a little boy waiting for his school bus. Wounded but determined, I would rush and tackle the madman. Cops would show up and arrest him, and then—and only then—I would gracefully pass out. Naturally, I would wake up in the hospital, looking slightly peaked in a ravishing way, to find my room filled with family and friends and the mayor and the press. I would be modest about my heroism—everyone would be charmed and then they would clear out and my mother would lean over and say that there was someone special to see me. She would split, and in would walk my rock star—humble, emotional, eyes brimming with tears in a manly way. It would turn out that the little boy whose life I saved was the musician's beloved younger brother. Mr. Musician would have realized that I am the greatest person he's ever met and his enormous mistake at ditching me. It would turn out that he was already on his way back for me even before the shooting incident but this really clinched it, and now his entire family was rooting for us to spend the rest of our lives together. My injury would of course not be life-threatening but would leave an extremely sexy scar. I played this one out so many times in my head that I think my "fantasy me" was starting to look like Swiss cheese with all the bullets I'd taken.

Lucy's reconciliation fantasy involved tragedy for her ex. Something terrible would happen in his life like the death of someone close to him or the destruction of his beloved truck, and this event would make him realize what a fool he'd been. Like in the movies, Lucy's ex would show up at her office with a bunch of flowers, weeping, and looking as if he hadn't slept in a month. He would beg her forgiveness and say all the things that she'd ever wanted him to say but that he never had, like "I need you" and "I can't live without you." Needless to say, Lucy would take the rest of the day off so that the two of them could cry and cry and laugh and talk and promise that they'd never split up again.

It's also absolutely essential to keep in mind that your ex, even if he initiated the breakup, is having some fantasies—or nightmares—of his own these days. And if he's like most males, his fantasies are all about his insecurities. You may be sitting at home weeping, but your ex doesn't know that and no doubt he's going to imagine what he fears most, just as you have feared that about him. Take a few minutes to relish the fact that men are so territorial and competitive about women and everything else that your ex is probably imagining that you are sharing your charms with a wealthier and taller man who drives an expensive car, lives in a mansion, is self-made, and is hung like a stallion. You are not the only one with an imagination, and who knows? Maybe all your ex's fears will be realized in the next man in your life.

VISION OF A LIFE

Processing a breakup often means not only grieving for the relationship that you and your ex had but also mourning the loss of what I call "a vision of a life." This is extremely common. While it might not make you feel terrific, it's important to reclaim some parts of the "vision of life" that you had and make them belong to you again and return them to a vision of *your* future. Only parts of the vision need be lost with the man in question.

For example, when Samantha's boyfriend broke up with her, Samantha was sad that her ex was no longer in her life but also brokenhearted that they would never have the life together that she had imagined. In Samantha's case, her vision of her life with her ex included a small wedding in Hawaii, having a daughter they would name Alice, a trip to Paris, a house with a small backyard in the suburbs, golf vacations, among other things. Some parts of Samantha's vision were things that she and her ex had discussed (Paris, the house, golf) and some were things that Samantha had thought that a future with her ex might happily and reasonably include (Hawaiian wedding, Alice). After the breakup, Samantha was experiencing the loss of all the things she and her ex said they would do, and all the things that she had hoped they would. Samantha was overwhelmed with sadness, so she decided to write down everything that had been part of the vision of a life she had for her and her ex. Samantha made five lists: (1) things in the vision that she still wanted to do that she could do alone or with friends; (2) things in the vision that she still wanted to do in a couple someday; (3) things that she had only wanted to do with her ex; (4) things that she had accepted but actually didn't really want in her future; and (5) things that she could never have had in a future with her ex but that she could now throw back into the mix.

In the end, Samantha realized that there were a lot of things in the vision that she had accepted when she was with her ex but actually weren't what she personally wanted. For example, she realized that she would much rather live in the city than the suburbs. She could still have a small wedding in Hawaii someday and could still have a daughter named Alice. She could easily spend more time golfing with friends, starting immediately. And she actually wasn't that jazzed about going to Paris but she and her ex had settled on it because he wasn't a very adventurous traveler. Actually, she really wanted to go to India and Morocco and decided that she might well meet a new man who was more like-minded about travel. And if she didn't, she might just have to get a friend to go with her. Suddenly, she was realizing that there were a lot of things that she would have had to give up if she'd spent the rest of her life with her ex that she didn't want to give up. This exercise not only gave Samantha a sense that there were many aspects of the vision of the life that she'd had with her ex that weren't disappearing with him but also made her realize that she was now free to chuck the things that weren't her cup of tea. It gave Samantha a slightly better sense of what she wanted from life and what kind of man she wanted to share it with down the road.

Why not give it a whirl?

SHAME

Unfortunately, almost every woman I know has felt some measure of shame or at least embarrassment about the fact someone broke up with her. Of course, on a personal level, rejection is uncomfortable and painful and can feel like a whopping critique of one's worth. But it seems to me that our culture is much more likely to hold women responsible for their heartbreaks than it does men. It seems that many people have stereotypes about men and women that make rejection somehow more damning for a woman. Many women are taught that it is our goal to get a man to commit to us, and many men are taught that's is normal for them to want to avoid that commitment. Of course, both of these social messages are uncool and do a disservice to us all. But the result of these stereotypes is that when a man breaks up with a woman, she may be made to feel that she has failed at her "goal," while when a woman breaks up with a man, on some level, he is made to feel that he is somehow lucky to have escaped a close call with the commitment he should have been trying to avoid. Let me give you an example. On countless occasions when I was asked if I had a boyfriend and I replied no, the follow-up question was "Why not?" or "What's wrong with you?" In all his life my brother has never been asked "what's wrong" with him when he told someone he didn't have a girlfriend.

Anyway, if you are feeling some measure of shame that you've been rejected, you should know that it's somewhat normal and that every woman from your grandmother to Nicole Kidman has experienced it. On a different note, keep in mind that the fact that your ex broke up with you is as much or more about him than it is about you, and you should try not to let unfair stereotypes make you feel any worse than you already do.

This is, obviously, a lot easier said than done. But the thing about stereotypes is that we all create them, and we often come to believe them even though they can be hurtful to us and not especially true. If the stereotype above sounded silly but also tugged at you because part of you believes it, you need to take a little time to think about it. It's simply not good—even destructive—for you to go around having any part of you believing something that is toxic, internally and in terms of the way you interact with the world. What are the experiences or observations that may have led you to believe that, as women, our "goal" is to get a man to commit to us? What are your experiences or observations that may have led you to believe that men are "commitmentphobic"? All of your observations or experiences may be "real," but what are your thoughts? What are the women like whom you most admire? The men? How does their behavior match up with these stereotypes?

The bottom line is that while you may not be able to control how the rest of the world thinks, you can control how you do. Always remember, if there was nothing "wrong" with you two months ago before the breakup, hello, there's nothing wrong with you now.

BLAMING YOURSELF

Every woman I know after thinking and thinking about a relationship that ended painfully has tried—in one way or another—to take the blame for it ending. I can't count how many times a friend has said, "Maybe if I'd been more compassionate about this or that . . ." or "If I hadn't had to work such long hours . . ." or "If I had never mentioned that I want to have children . . ." The bottom line is that when a man really loves you and wants to be in a relationship, no one comment or incident is ever the reason the relationship ends. There are a lot of ways to deal with issues or differences of opinion in a relationship that don't involve breaking up.

Furthermore, nobody is perfect. No doubt your ex had many flaws himself. So why should you expect yourself to be flawless? So maybe you weren't always a bowl of laughs, but who is? Whatever you were doing, you were being yourself. It may be that there are some things about you that you'd like to change, but there is no reason that they couldn't have been worked on in the context of the relationship.

BLAMING HIM

The obvious flip side of blaming yourself for the breakup is blaming your ex. And initially, as I recommended in different ways earlier, it was a good idea to throw the blame his way. He did break up with you, so technically he was responsible. And blaming him was a whole lot better than blaming yourself. Whether or not he was a huge jerk, he did hurt you and you needed to be angry at him. It was really important to say those horrible things about him to your friends and to write them down. It was important to get clear on all your ex's shortcomings and to remind yourself of how great you are.

But after a while, blame is boring. It's possible that your ex—during the relationship or in the end—did some horrible things. It's possible that your ex was truly responsible for the relationship not working. And I'm not suggesting that you have to forgive him. But even if your ex was a nightmare, you don't want to get rutted in the role of victim. It's not good for your self-esteem and it's just not becoming.

Also, ongoing strong feelings of blame or anger toward your ex may mean that you are still more emotionally connected to him than is good for you. If you can't break away from thinking about whose fault the relationship ending was, you may be trying to avoid coming to terms with the fact that the relationship is over. Sometimes when you put a lot of energy into blame issues, you may, on some level, be holding on to the idea that if you could solve the mystery you and your ex could be together again. For better or worse, that is simply not true.

BEYOND BLAME

Blaming yourself and blaming your ex for things not working out are normal phases in your recovery. But, as I've outlined above, they have limited usefulness, and sooner rather than later you want to move beyond both. Given that the relationship is over, it's much more useful to look at *yourself* in a blame-free way and try to figure out who you were in the relationship, whether you have any unhealthy relationship patterns, and whether there are things that hold you back from the full enjoyment of your life or future relationships.

Samantha

Samantha and Scott went out for two years. Scott dropped hints throughout their relationship that he wasn't sure that he wanted to have the kind of committed relationship with possible marriage that Samantha said she did, and yet she continued to go out with him. After their breakup, Samantha decided that it was a good time to take a look at herself and discovered some painful but important things. Samantha had always thought—without really thinking about it—that she wanted to get married and have a family. Yet it became clear to her that she always picked men who were unavailable in some way or another. Before Scott, she'd had two extremely long-distance relationships and a relationship with a married man. And then there was Scott who had flat-out said he wasn't going to be available long term. Why would this be? After a lot of thinking, Samantha realized that, in fact, *she* had some very ambivalent feelings about commitment and marriage. Her parents had a really troubled relationship and her mother bore the brunt of it. Samantha discovered that she harbored intense fears about getting married and had been deliberately trying to avoid her mother's fate by only going out with men who were very unlikely candidates for the altar. She realized that if she ever did want to get married or start dating men who might want to get married, she was going to do some work on her own fears first.

Holly

When Holly and Mark broke up, Holly was distraught. She had spent the past two years of her life focusing all her time and attention on Mark. They never really talked about Holly or her needs. Holly, in fact, made it seem that she had no needs at all. In one of their final conversations, Mark told Holly that he felt as if he didn't even know her. Holly was stunned but, over time, as she began healing, she realized that in a way Mark had been right. There were a lot of things that she had avoided telling Mark because she was worried that he might be put off by them and, in her fear of losing him, she had never really let him get to know her. Maybe even more important, Holly realized that she had focused so much attention and energy on Mark because she had herself wanted to avoid coming to terms with some painful issues in her past.

When Holly was in high school, she had cancer. She spent a year out of school getting treatment and recuperating at home. Holly's parents made her feel that her illness was something to be ashamed of. They lied to her school about why she was out and they forbade her to tell anyone or see any of her friends until her hair had grown back and she looked like her former self. The cancer was in itself very traumatic for Holly, as was the way her parents handled it. Sadly, though, their behavior was consistent with their more general and overwhelming concern with the appearance of being "normal," even perfect. As a result, Holly had always done her best to be "perfect," excelling at school and at work and trying to be what she understood was perfect in a relationship. After the breakup with Mark, Holly started to reconsider her parents' values and the immense pressure that she'd always put on herself. Over time, she started to be much more compassionate with herself. She realized that she had to learn to love and accept herself before she could comfortably share herself with someone else and let him love her too.

Lucy

When David and Lucy broke up, all of her friends—including me—were very relieved. We were sad that Lucy was heartbroken but happy that she would not be spending one more second with a man who treated her like a doormat. On top of being horrible to Lucy, David was irresponsible, obnoxious, ignorant, and lazy. Many of Lucy's friends were completely stunned that Lucy would even have gone out with David to begin with. True, none of Lucy's boyfriends had ever seemed like her equals, but David was the worst. It took Lucy a while to realize on her own how inappropriate for her David had been, and when she did, she decided it was a good idea to explore how she ended up in such an unhealthy relationship and why she always seemed to get involved with men whom no one thought were good enough for her. It was the first time that Lucy thought seriously about the fact that her mother had abandoned her and her sisters when they were children. It had always been there, a fact of her life, but she'd never considered that it might have deep implications in terms of her relationships as a grown-up. Over time, Lucy realized that her mother's actions had really compromised Lucy's self-esteem. She dated men who were unkind to her or simply not good enough for her because, on some level, she felt she wasn't worthy of more. If her own mother had abandoned her, certainly she wasn't lovable. The incredible thing about this situation from an outsider's perspective is that everyone who knows Lucy thinks she is amazing. She is kind, funny, successful, and smart. And yet deep down Lucy couldn't see what was so clear to the rest of us. Lucy decided that she needed to focus some time and energy on addressing and healing from the emotional wound her mother had inflicted on her by leaving. And she realized that in the future she needed to avoid picking shabby men based on her own sometimes shaky self-esteem.

Emily

Emily has had both good and not-so-good relationships. But what stood out for her when she and Tim broke up was that she almost always had a boyfriend, and she spent a disproportionate amount of time in each relationship focusing on the other person. What had been obvious to some of her girlfriends but was clear to her only in hindsight was that she was using relationships as a way to avoid dealing with some of her own issues. In particular, Emily always wanted to be a doctor. Her family discouraged her interest because they felt that she showed little aptitude for math and science. For about ten years after college, Emily flirted with several professions but never really felt satisfied with what she was doing. In that decade, however, she had five serious relationships and helped many of her boyfriends move ahead with their goals. Finally, after Tim left, Emily decided that it was time to focus on herself. She realized that she had been afraid to try premed classes because she had built up a great fear of failure and of disappointing her parents. Eventually, Emily got the courage up to take one class; she didn't ace it, but she did fine. She's applying to medical schools this fall.

You

None of the above examples may sound familiar to you. But if there are some things inside you that hamper you from being your best—alone and in future relationships—I hope they get you thinking.

It's incredibly common for people to use relationships as a way to avoid taking a good look at themselves. It's also quite common for people to lay blame for not fulfilling their own potential on others, usually on the people closest to them. We often play out childhood issues or traumas in our current relationships. Obviously, in the above examples that was true and wasn't a good thing. Of course, not all childhood experiences are negative. If your father was extremely devoted to you and you are interested in having children, you may want to meet someone who shares some of the same positive qualities your father had.

I am in no way suggesting that you have to be alone to work on these kinds of issues. You may find yourself in a relationship again soon, and you may work on your emotional growth while you are in it. In the meantime, however, the more you do to make yourself the best you can be emotionally, the better your chances are of finding a healthy relationship and making it work. Also, the better you will feel in general.

RELATIONSHIP PATTERNS: SOME QUESTIONS

1. Grab a piece of paper and list all the boyfriends you have had. Next to each one, jot down some adjectives that best describe him. Do you see any similarities among the men in your past? If so, are those similarities positive or negative, in your opinion? What do they reflect about you?

2. Now consider each of these relationships in terms of yourself. Describe who you were in each relationship. Were you the same person in each relationship? If so, how? If not, how do you feel you were different and why?

3. Do the roles that you played in these relationships reflect how you think of yourself as an individual? If so, how? If not, how?

4. Do the roles you played in these relationships reflect how others (friends, family, etc.) think of you? If so, how? If not, how?

5. Do you like the person you were in your different relationships? What, if anything, might you change? What do you feel good about?

BEING SINGLE

It will probably take you some time to think of yourself as being single. For some people it helps to say it out loud; it starts to make it feel real. For others, saying it out loud before you've digested it in your head is just too painful (not that you should lie if asked, just dodge). Becoming single again is similar to being alone again in that it takes time to process, and you may find that sometimes you've forgotten that you are single and then it comes back to you and feels like a ton of bricks crashing on your head. Obviously, big changes take some time to get used to.

Being single can be awesome if it's what you want or sometimes even when it's not what you want long term. But in order to enjoy it you have to get comfortable with it. No matter how you slice it, being single means more freedom. Let's consider what's potentially frightening about that and what's great about it.

Solo Downside

The following statements may not have actually been true in your recent relationship, or perhaps were only partially true but, like most of us, you may feel in romanticized hindsight that they were.

✿   Having a boyfriend can sometimes feel like a shield (even if he's scrawny). Being part of a couple can feel like protection when dealing with unpleasant colleagues, maddening family members, rude neighbors, lecherous men. It can feel as if others know that if they cross or hurt you, they may have someone else to contend with. Or you may feel that having a boyfriend lessens the degree to which others can affect you.

✿   If you don't have a lot of close male friends or brothers (or maybe even if you do), being part of a couple can make you feel more comfortable or more confident with men in general. You know you're taken; they know you're taken. Because you are less self-conscious of how these other men perceive you, you may feel more comfortable acting like yourself. Or you may feel that having a boyfriend is a sign that you are attractive, which makes you more confident in your dealings with other men (this is probably something learned, something cultural, and *not* a good thing).

✿   Being part of a couple can give you a way out of dealing with social obligations that you would rather not deal with. For example, if you'd like to skip your cousin's wedding and you try the excuse that it's your friend's birthday that day, it probably won't fly well. But if you say it's your boyfriend's parents' anniversary party, people are more likely to let it slide. Additionally, it gives you someone to blame when you don't want to do something so you are not the bad guy but rather just a harried, loving girlfriend.

Before we get to the more positive aspects of being single, let's talk about the above. Having a man in your life *can* be a shield from the irritation or injustices that you may experience in the world. You have someone to whom you can probably turn when the rest of the world doesn't seem that hospitable, and perhaps someone who others think can do a better job at kicking their ass than you can. But on the flip side, you, as a loving partner, may feel the vulnerabilities of your man. For example, if your boyfriend is having a very rough patch in his career or is beginning a new career, it may make you feel insecure or even defensive. I'm not saying that you are the kind of superficial person who jumps ship when the going gets tough, but sometimes when the going gets tough in your man's life, you feel extra-exposed as well. It's normal, but in those times, you may not feel that your man can do much "shielding" for you. Being single, you may have to face the world with your own vulnerabilities, but you don't face the world with anyone else's.

As for being more comfortable and confident with the opposite sex, you may or may not have experienced this, but if you did, it's not necessarily something that you lose entirely when your ex walks out that door. Not to sound trite, but if you've felt something once, you can feel it again. Part of the experience of feeling more confident with other men may be related to the stereotypes that I talked about earlier and isn't something you can do on your own: You can't necessarily change how narrow-minded or even well-intentioned narrow-minded people view you. But you can try to hold on to the feeling that you can act completely like yourself and have good interactions with men—men you'd like to be just friends with and men you could potentially be interested in.

It's nice to have someone who, by his mere existence, helps you create boundaries with others. But in the scheme of life, it's much much better to be someone who can say no on your own to social (and work) demands on your time. It's better because it can serve you in your next relationship when you need to make sure that you are as giving to yourself as you are to your partner. It's better because it means that you know how to take respectful and loving care of yourself. It's better because the more honest you are with people who make unreasonable demands on your time, the less negative feelings you harbor about them. And, honey, it's a very necessary skill for right now because people often assume that when you are single they can make greater demands on your time than when you are in a couple, and that may not work for you at all. (Why would you want to spend the entire weekend helping an annoying colleague move into a new apartment when you wouldn't have before?)

Solo Upside

It may not feel that there are many upsides to being single right now, but there are. You may not feel like embracing them yet, but remember that just because you embrace them now and maximize your single experience, it doesn't mean you have to embrace them permanently.

✿ Every close relationship involves compromise. When you are not in one, obviously you don't have to make those compromises. From the little things (you love Chinese food, he can't even stand the smell of it) to big things (you are living in a town that you hate where you have no family and few friends because that's where his job is), you may have had to concede on a lot of things that weren't great for you. Now you can do what you want.

✿ You no longer have to worry about someone else's schedule or mood or health or career or family or problems. You probably spent a lot of energy and time and thought (and maybe even money) on your ex. As you know, this can be very draining even when things are going well. Your ex was quite possibly not worthy of it. Now that you are single, you can lavish the energy, time, and thought on yourself and making your life better, and on the other people in your life who definitely deserve it.

✿ Another exciting thing about being single again is that you may now meet a man who is better for you, who requires you to make fewer compromises or different compromises that feel more appropriate for you.

If you want to, you will end up in a loving, committed relationship at some point. Right now, that may seem like exactly what you want. But keep in mind if you are thirty-three today and the average American woman lives until she is eighty or so, you may be looking at fifty years with the same man, the same body. Now, there are many potentially wonderful things about that, but let's be honest, it's a *really* long time. It's so long that it's actually hard to get one's mind around. In the scheme of life, what's an extra six months or year or two as a single woman? Because unless you get divorced, you will never ever be single again, you will never experience the initial excitement of falling in love and acting on it. As incredible as the man you end up with will be, you won't get butterflies every time his arm brushes yours. That can happen only in the beginning. Being single, you know that you will get to have that experience at least one more time.

CHANGE OF POV

Lucy has a brilliant writing exercise for times when she's been in postbreakup mode and feels as if she's gotten her head a little stuck up her arse and on her ex. Grab your "breakup" notebook and write about the relationship and the breakup from the perspective of someone else—an imaginary friend/narrator. I've tried it and it's been helpful to me (and will, I hope, be the basis of a novel if I can ever find those notes).

Because you were in love with your ex, you have a charming lack of objectivity on the whole situation. As I've discussed, your real friends may have already clued you in as to what it was like to witness some of it without being in love with your ex. But there may be some things they don't know because you didn't want to tell them. Or maybe they know every gory detail. It doesn't matter: You are you, not them. And it may help you get things in perspective to write about it all as if you weren't you. You may even recognize some similarities your relationship had with a romance a friend of yours had that you had hoped would end. Take a crack at it. You have nothing to lose.

MEMORIES

It's always easier to remember the good times that you had with your ex when you are feeling sentimental about the relationship. But it's wise to get a more balanced and realistic grip on that relationship and remember that it had some painful times too, even before it ended. Write out some of the good memories and some of the bad memories. You shouldn't have to work too hard to create a list that isn't ridiculously lopsided toward the good memories. This exercise isn't intended to make you realize that the relationship sucked—it may not have—but just to keep ya from romanticizing it. It's helpful to keep this list handy for times that you feel you are drifting into the land of retroactive soft focus.

ON THE MORE POSITIVE SIDE . . .

It's also healthy at some point to consider what you got, besides heartbreak, from your relationship. You probably had some good experiences or learned some new things while you were with your ex that will always be with you. Even if your sadness doesn't make them seem worth it, it's important to know that you're not leaving this relationship completely empty-handed.

For example, Josie moved to Portland to follow her boyfriend who was relocating to a new job. They ended up breaking up, but Josie would have never moved to Portland if it hadn't been for her ex, and she loves it there. Emily never felt comfortable with her body until she met her ex. For all his other flaws, he made Emily feel that her body is beautiful, and she is more confident for having been with him. Lucy, whose Parisian ex wasn't a great match for her, learned to speak French fluently. One of my exes left me with the important and clear knowledge that I hate both mosh pits and cockfights.

Grab some paper and write down anything you got out of your last relationship, even if it's just things that you realized about yourself.

COUPLES, COUPLES EVERYWHERE

The way the mind works, you notice things that mean something to you. So if you are suddenly single, you may also find yourself suddenly noticing couples everywhere doing coupley things that depress you. You may also find that you are suddenly noticing single women who seem unhappy. It's normal that you are extrasensitive right now, but remember that the world at large is no different from the way it was a few months ago; you are just extra-aware of anything that seems connected to your current feelings. You may have noticed this phenomenon before. Someone tells you that she has some medical condition, for example. Suddenly it seems that news about that medical condition is in every newspaper you pick up. Then two other people mention that they have the same problem and so on and so on. When your sensibilities are heightened to something, you will see it everywhere. It's normal, but it doesn't mean that the world is trying to send you a message or that something freaky is happening. It's just your tenderness and it will pass. If you are feeling oppressed by how often you are now noticing things that make you blue, try to sharpen your focus on the world around you. Make an effort to observe the vast majority of things going on out there that don't reinforce or trigger sad feelings or feel personal. Even if it makes the world seem more impersonal, it will remind you that sometimes the world's indifference to your feelings can be reassuring.

part two: TEMPTATIONS AND REALITIES RELATED TO YOUR EX

Most likely your ex has not disappeared off the face of the earth and even more likely he's still on your mind. Let's look at a few topics related to him that may be cropping up.

THE SLIPPERY SLOPE: BEING IN TOUCH

It's been a month, and you may be thinking, wouldn't it be harmless to just call him up and say hi? Just a little contact to see if you can tell if he's missing you or if he sounds like crap? This is where I ask you to keep in mind a very wise blues refrain: "Don't let the same dog bite you twice."

Let's briefly examine an experience of Hannah's. She was madly in love with and going out with this guy for about a year. He'd dropped hints all the way through that he wasn't sure if he could imagine sharing the rest of his life with someone because he felt that he didn't have much to offer. (And, having met him, let me just say that he was 100 percent right.) Anyway, Hannah devoted herself to making him feel worthy, to helping him get a better apartment, to helping him find a new job—all in the hopes that his self-esteem would improve and he would realize just what a wonderful person he was, what a wonderful husband he'd make for someone like Hannah. (Already this was on the wrong track . . .) In the end, it didn't work out. The guy dumped Hannah, saying that it was really for her own good because she deserved better. Hannah was devastated. And the truth is I think the guy was devastated. Hannah is the greatest. Who wouldn't want Hannah around, being loving and funny and upbeat? But when Hannah wanted a sense of whether this relationship had a potential future (moving in together, possible marriage, normal stuff), the guy realized that he might actually have to give something in return for Hannah's love, and he freaked. I feel confident that he would have been delighted to go out with Hannah indefinitely if she had had no expectations of him.

Cut to a month after Hannah and the Jerk (let's make things easier and give him a name) break up. Hannah calls him. She misses him, etc. The Jerk *is* happy to hear from Hannah and in fact he sounds terrible. He does miss Hannah, he does miss having her in his life. Hannah is just so happy that the Jerk still cares for her that she starts seeing him again. She assumes that if he wants to get back together, then he's thought more about the issues that were important to her and is ready to have the kind of relationship that Hannah had wanted before. Big mistake. One day about a month into them reconciling, Hannah invites the Jerk to a family function. She's not even thinking it's a big deal. Of course, it's really not a big deal but the Jerk had been thinking that if Hannah is getting back together with him then *she* understands that it is going to be a Hannah-gives-everything-but-has-no-expectations relationship. And the Jerk promptly broke up with Hannah again. Needless to say, it was horrible.

I'm not saying that one teeny call is going to lead to a situation like Hannah's. Hannah's may be the worst-case scenario, but none of them are good. Let's consider two others:

✿ He's fine. You call him up. You talk. He sounds fine. He's even friendly. You hang up and feel more miserable than you did before.

✿ No return. You call him. You leave a message. He doesn't call you back. You feel more miserable than you did before and you feel extranervous every time the phone rings.

The bottom line hasn't changed: If your ex has realized that he's madly in love with you and wants to get back together, he'll get in touch with you.

HE WANTS YOU BACK

You may be wishing for this desperately right now, and if he's not calling you, you may want to just skip this part lest you get more upset.

Let's say he gets in touch with you and he does want you back. It's not uncommon for a man who breaks your heart to realize he's made a terrible mistake and want to get back together. It actually happens a lot. And it can work out in many different ways. If you are going to even consider getting back together with your ex, here are some things to keep in mind.

✿ Talk to each other. Before you jump back in his arms and set yourself up to be hurt again, make sure that you are both totally clear on what happened to make the relationship end and what you both want from the relationship this time around. He may be missing you (who wouldn't?), but is he really ready to get into a relationship again? Does he acknowledge how much he's hurt you? Does he understand that he's broken your trust, and is he willing to help build that trust back? Is he going to be able to be patient with you if you are feeling insecure about the relationship for a while? If you find that your ex is getting squirmy just talking about these issues, he probably won't be able to handle the work you two would have to do to get back together in a balanced, trusting relationship.

✿ Listen carefully. Try to hear what he is saying to you. I know this sounds obvious, but it's very common when you want something badly not to concentrate on the fine print.

✿ In talking to your ex who apparently still loves you, it may seem that you could wipe out everything that's happened in the last month. But take a moment to ask yourself the following questions: Are you comfortable being with someone who has hurt you before? Do you think that you will be able to trust him again? Can you imagine yourself getting to a place in the relationship where you wouldn't feel insecure? Everyone has different answers to these questions, and some of them have to do with life experience. Josie, whose father had an affair that led to her parents' divorce, was torn when her ex wanted to get back together with her. She had a hard time trusting men to begin with. And in the end, though she still had feelings for her ex, she didn't feel that she'd be able to have the kind of relationship she wanted in the future with someone who had let her down so painfully already. Who knows if that was the right decision, but the bottom line is that it's important to think and talk about how you feel before you make your decision.

✿ I know it's hard, but go slow. You need to keep in mind that you have been through a lot and are still extremely fragile. If your ex really wants to be with you, what can it hurt not to have tons of sleepovers right away? If you are feeling a little skittish, that's completely understandable and don't pretend that you are not. If he wants you back, you two are going to have to rebuild a lot of trust, and that is a slow process. No relationships come with guarantees, and even if you and your ex seem to be on the same page and you have given getting back together a lot of thought, there is no harm in being a little cautious and self-protective on your way back into this relationship. In fact, your friends would probably slap you if you weren't.

✿ Finally, do the "vision of a life" exercise if you are thinking about getting back together with your ex. See how a future with and without your ex works out for you after you've had the experience of this past month.

COMPULSIVE COMMUNICATIONS CHECKING

You haven't heard from your ex. Maybe you've been in touch, maybe you haven't, but you find yourself calling in from work to check your messages at home about ninety-three times an hour. Or every time you go on-line for work, you check your personal E-mail. Or you find yourself stepping on your cat's head to get to the answering machine as you walk in the door to see if its light is blinking. With the possible exception of the cat, is there anyone who doesn't do this? It's insane *and* it's normal.

There isn't much to say about this except that over time you will find that you just aren't as concerned about the possible messages you may or may not be receiving. Just between me and myself however, I felt a little better when I put some limits on the checking of my messages because when I discovered (as I invariably did) that my ex hadn't called, a wave of disappointment and sadness would wash over me, and how many times a day did I need to feel that? So I would limit my calling in to my messages from work to once or twice a day. If you can do it, do it. You may feel a little pathetic, but it's less pathetic than calling in every three minutes. If you can't, who cares? In time, it'll just happen.

E-MAIL ETIQUETTE

You may be innocently checking your E-mail—compulsively or not—and have your heart skip a beat because there is an E-mail from your ex. You click to open it—your pulse quickening—only to discover that you are one of fifty people your ex has E-mailed regarding a petition to save dolphins or, worse, a joke. Yup, it's not pretty but it's a reality. E-mail lists with the accompanying impersonal messages abound, and it's quite possible that you are still on your ex's list. It's tacky and it's annoying even if you love dolphins, jokes, the environment, etc. And the most infuriating aspect of it is that most likely your ex doesn't even realize that you are still on his list. This is when you make a note to yourself to take any exes off your list. Then type a very simple—and ideally embarrassing for your ex—reply that goes like this: "I appreciate your concern for _____/

I appreciate that you find _____ humorous, but please take me off your E-mail list. Many thanks." Make it sound almost as if your assistant wrote it (even if you don't have one) or as if it's an automatic message that you have ingeniously programmed your computer to send when you receive asinine mass E-mails. It's that simple. Don't get personal. He didn't. But do reply without seeming too hostile and save yourself the anxiety of ever being duped into thinking that you are getting a personal E-mail from him when you aren't. Also, make sure that you are blocked from your ex's instant messaging list and vice versa. You definitely don't need extra temptation to dash off an E-mail you can't take back. And you don't need your ex to know every time you are on-line.

OTHER LIST ETIQUETTE

If you chronically—or even once—date a musician or a stand-up comic or an artist, you may find yourself with another kind of hassle. Those mailers that once seemed so endearing and made you hope that one day your man would be a big star will now drive you insane. It's one thing to imagine that your ex is still at his office sending E-mails, but to have constant reminders that he is continuing to be out there performing or showing his art when he should be home grieving is distressing. As I've learned from experience, it can be particularly depressing when these mailers are announcing larger and larger venues and album releases from which you can deduce that more and possibly hotter groupies are hanging around backstage draped over your ex with bare midriff . . . I digress. The point is that this is a real drag and you may or may not have an easy way to handle the situation. If your ex makes his own fliers and sends them out to a list himself, just E-mail him or leave him a simple message asking him to remove you from the list. Don't use this as an opportunity to leave a long nasty message. Another way to go—especially if your ex has management that handles his lists—is simply to send the flier back to sender marked "addressee unknown." Soon enough, someone should be updating those lists and you should stop receiving the mailings. Under no circumstances—even if you've never looked better— should you attend the opening/show/whatever.

STALKING OR EVEN THE CASUAL WALK-BY

Obviously, stalking is a no-no. Not only is it illegal but it's beneath you. If you are going to your ex's haunts, his office, or his home without invitation, you have a serious problem and you must—*must*—must get help right away. Additionally, stalking has never ever, not once ever, made a person change his or her mind about a breakup. I daresay that stalking only pushes someone farther away from his or her ex. I once had a boyfriend who tried to get a job at my office after we broke up. He didn't get the job, but he did scare me and I carried scissors in my purse for a couple of weeks.

If you are like me and my friends, stalking is too desperate for you, but the drive-by or the walk-by is tempting. Maybe you want to see if he's home. Or you are secretly hoping for a run-in during which your ex will drop to his knees sobbing and apologizing. What can I say? Almost everyone I know has "casually" strolled by the ex's pad or favorite bar with a racing pulse. Obviously, it's not a good idea, and as we can all attest nothing romantic has ever come of this kind of behavior. Josie once did catch a glimpse of an ex hand in hand with the tart he dumped her for on their way out to a formal. Curious as she was about the new woman, the vision of this peroxide blonde in a see-through dress on her ex's arm did not make her feel better and unfortunately remained etched in her mind for some time. Holly used to drive past her ex's all the time and call me from her cell phone asking me if she should get out of her car and just "drop by." About ten seconds after meeting her new boyfriend, it seems that she forgot where her ex even lived.

If you can control yourself, just don't do it. If you are going to do it, drive by—never walk—even if it means taking a taxi. This lessens the chance of an actual face-to-face encounter (which is really for the best) and makes you far less vulnerable, especially if you live in a place where there will be no other pedestrians to blend in with.

part three: PLUGGING BACK IN

If you haven't already, you need to start reconnecting socially with the world around you. The good news is that you can do it at a pace that feels comfortable to you—you don't have to go hog-wild or anything. The bad news is that if nothing feels comfortable, you actually do have to force yourself to do a few small things to get back in the mix. They can be tiny little baby steps involving only people you really love, so don't be alarmed. Also, you need to continue to take excellent care of yourself— or start to, if you weren't ready to earlier.

INVITATIONS: RECEIVING, ACCEPTING, AND MAKING

Even if you are not ready to accept every invitation out there right now, you want to put yourself on everyone's invitation radar screen. Basically this means letting your close friends know that they should keep you posted on any events they know about and they should tell their friends—much like those old shampoo commercials—that you are back in the mix. And you should make an effort to accept some of the invitations that come your way.

Whether or not you are getting lots of invitations from friends who are very social, it's time for you to start extending an invitation or two. At the very least, get your girlfriends together at your house for dinner sometime soon. They may not all know each other, or some may not even like each other that much, but they all love you and want you to feel loved and protected when you've been feeling lousy. Additionally, none of them will care about how fancy a meal you serve or how snazzy your house looks. But if you still haven't gotten around to tidying up a bit, maybe having people over is just the motivation you need.

HOW TO EXPLAIN THE BREAKUP

You may begin to find these days that it comes up here and there that you've recently been through a breakup. Perhaps you are at a social function and realize, to your horror, that a tactless friend or relative is telling someone who then turns to you, also tactlessly, to ask you about it. Or you may yourself occasionally mention the breakup to someone whom you didn't feel like telling before or didn't run into when it first happened or even whom you want to know that you are now available. People will invariably ask you what happened. You need to find a comfortable way to answer that question or tactfully avoid answering it. You are obviously always within your rights to say that you'd rather not talk about it, though this might be a little awkward if you yourself brought it up.

You don't want to seem too emotional or too bitter about the breakup, particularly when you are dealing with people whom you do not know that well or who may be a source of interesting dates down the road. Of course, we all have a moment now and then when we spontaneously burst into tears or blurt out that our ex is a f—king asshole. (These moments happened to me more frequently when I'd had several cocktails . . .) If you can avoid having many moments like this, you probably will feel better the next morning or the next time you run into the person on the receiving end of your mini-outburst.

When you are interacting with people you don't know well, keep in mind that you are under no, none, nada obligation to tell them the exact truth about who broke up with whom. There is just no need for it. Why make yourself feel vulnerable with people who aren't your close friends and family? You wouldn't tell them the specifics about anything else really private in your life, so why should divulge this? Unless you live in a really small town (and even if you do), it's rock solid, in my opinion, simply to say, "We didn't want the same things." People can interpret that however they want, but I think it's totally dignified and, in fact, it's 100 percent true. That's just about the right amount of information for someone you don't know well to be privy to anyway. If you want or feel the need to say more, stay general and don't mention anything that is really loaded for you. For example, you could throw in something like, "We just had different ideas about how we wanted to spend our time" or "We didn't have as much in common as we initially thought." Staying vague is good, though if you are feeling bitchy and are talking to someone who doesn't know your ex and isn't likely ever to meet him, it might be amusing to get a little creative. You could say, for example, that your volunteer work with homeless children is so important to you and you felt it wasn't right for your ex to ask you to drop it. Or you could hint at some problems that your ex had of an intimate nature that you and he worked on together but just couldn't be solved. Or you could say that you and your ex had some concerns about his sexual orientation . . . I suppose that this kind of lying could also be fun when talking with someone who does know your ex, but it's a little immature and probably beneath you. Spreading rumors at this point is tacky and could, of course, come back at you unpleasantly down the line.

DATING

Because time has probably passed faster for your close friends and family than it has for you recently, they may be expecting you to be out dating again. With or without your consent, they may have even lined up several dates for you. You should do whatever feels right for you when it comes to going out with new men. If you can't imagine anything more horrific than being out with someone new, then clearly you should skip it at least for the next few weeks or months. If people are trying to set you up, say that you really appreciate it and soon you will be ready and will let them know. You don't want to cut off any future opportunities just because you are not there yet. However, if you feel that you are ready to start dating again, go on with your bad self. You may want to keep the following in mind, but you know yourself better than I do so don't let these thoughts bring you down.

❧ It's totally normal to feel freaked out during or after a night spent in the company of a new man. It's also totally normal to come home and feel weird. Even if your new date was fantastic, he is not your ex (which is definitely a good thing). And, as you may remember from the last time you transitioned from being in a relationship to dating again, this can be unsettling.

✿ It's quite likely that part of you is still gun-shy. On some level, you may be frightened by the possibility of being hurt again. That's totally normal too, and if you begin dating fairly soon after your breakup, you should stay aware of what you are bringing into this dating situation. While it's good to be self-protective, it's very hard to get into a new relationship if you are not ready to trust again. Maybe this new guy is just the best person ever who makes you feel fantastic. Maybe you aren't sure how you feel about him. But if you like him and want to keep seeing him, it can't hurt to try to take things a little slowly. You should give yourself time to balance being in something new and slowly letting go of some of the emotional baggage that you are likely to be carrying around right now.

✿ You may be inclined to talk about your ex when you start dating again. You and your date may do the familiar dance at one point in the evening of swapping romantic histories. Regardless of what the ladies who wrote *The Rules* might dictate, there are no rules for this kind of situation. I think we both realize that getting really worked up about your ex in either anger or sadness is not good. You don't want to hurt your new date's feelings and, if he's interesting, you don't want him to think that he should wait several years before calling you again. It's also not great to make yourself really vulnerable with someone you don't know well. So if it comes up, address the breakup the same way you would with anyone else you don't know well and lay the "we didn't want the same things" on your date. If he asks you what you want, which he probably will, be as honest as you should be with anyone you don't know well. If you really want children someday, mention it. For chrissakes, if the guy is such a conceited jerk that he thinks you want his kids when you don't even know him, then he's a big loser anyway. Mention some other things that were important to you in the "vision of a life." Be yourself. How much of your dating life do you want to spend bullshitting and manipulating? It's exhausting and retro and pathetic. Who wants to end up with someone because you "tricked" him into wanting to be with a "you" that isn't really you?

FANCY A SHAG, BABY?

Getting a little rebound nookie can be a liberating thing at some point after a breakup. When exactly is, of course, extremely personal. It's probably a good call to keep in mind that premature postbreakup nookie can be really upsetting and I recommend giving it a little extra thought before you leap into the sack. If you are the kind of person who never has intimate relationships with men you don't know very well, then now is probably not the best time to check out what a one-night stand is like. Even if you've had your share of one-night stands before your recent relationship, the contrast between what it felt like then and what it feels like now coming off the heels of the relationship may not be that cool.

It may seem obvious, but never ever let peer pressure of any kind push you into getting into an intimate situation with a guy. Sometimes well-meaning friends suggest that a little nookie will help you "get over" your ex. They may be right, but the most important piece of it is that it will be "helpful" only when you are ready.

And finally, but most important, be SAFE. SAFE SEX, SAFE SEX, SAFE SEX. It's easy when your self-esteem is a little low to behave more recklessly than you might normally. But it would be a terrible thing if that led to an unwanted pregnancy, AIDS, or an STD of any kind that you might have for the rest of your life. If you are feeling frisky, make sure that you have condoms around *and* make sure that you use them. (If you don't feel up to buying condoms at your local corner store, order them from the superdiscreet folks at www.condomsexpress.com.)

RECYCLING MEN

I read in some magazine that it's a good idea to call all the men who have been interested in you in the past but you rejected and have them take you out to boost your morale when you are in postbreakup mode. As Emily pointed out when I mentioned the article to her, who has a lot of these people handy? Excellent question. If you've been in a serious relationship for a while, you may have to dig deep to find someone who you think may still have a crush on you, and it's totally unacceptable to track down the guy you declined to go to junior prom with. Lucy did try this once. She called a guy she had gently turned down a year earlier shortly after her boyfriend left. When he told her that he would love to get together and would like Lucy to meet his fiancée, she decided that this tactic for boosting morale was for the birds.

Here are my thoughts: Why would you call someone to get together whom you weren't interested in before? It's one thing to go on a date with someone new and realize that you are not interested in him—at least there was a chance that you would be. Calling old rejects or even old flames who somehow petered out is really a waste of time and is also likely to make you blue. Unlike paper and empties, men do not recycle well. If you had a strong feeling that a man wasn't right for you the first time, he's not going to be the right person for you now, and why would you feel better being reminded of that? Also, remember that it probably took any man you rejected some time to get over you. It's just mean to put him through it again.

There is, of course, one solid exception to this scenario. If there is a man you have known for a long time who always makes you feel good about yourself and is extremely attractive, single, and lives not too far away, but you are not seriously interested in and has no associations with your ex, you may want to dial him up immediately.

OTHER SINGLE WOMEN

It's quite possible that many of your girlfriends are in relationships. As you know from your own experience, single women are a moving target—one minute they are single, the next minute they are not. This may not seem important to you. You love your girlfriends who are not single. Why would you need other friends?

The thing is that it's always important to have friends who are experiencing life similarly to the way you are and who want to do the kinds of things you want to do. It's important to have friends who are available to hang out on Friday and Saturday nights. And it may be important to have friends who want to go to more "single-oriented" places.

I'm not suggesting that you blindly go out and make friends with just any women who are single. That would be like recommending that you move in on people with brown hair. But you might want to take a look around you and see if there are some single women in your orbit who might make terrific new friends.

STRENGTH IN NUMBERS

Especially since most people don't live near their immediate family, it's really nice to have a group of people you see regularly who care about you. I'm not suggesting that you cozy up to the barflies at the dive around the corner, but you might look to be a part of a group of friends who see each other on a regular basis if you are not already a part of one. It's good—single or not—to have a virtual family even if you are not superclose to all its members.

You may not think of yourself as a group person. You may prefer to have individual friendships that are really close. But it's not an either-or proposition. You can have lots of close friends *and* be part of a group of friends. In fact, maybe your friends would get along great and it's as simple as bringing them together.

Hannah has a bunch of friends who have a standing date for the third Friday of every month. They usually meet and hang out at a local coffeehouse, but sometimes they go elsewhere—to hear music, to go dancing. Lucy and her girlfriends get together for brunch the second Sunday of every month. Lucy says that the brunches make her feel as if she has her own little family in the middle of a huge, sometimes impersonal-feeling city.

I have other friends who play poker or mahjong with the same crew at different people's homes every month, which is great if you are into these games. The bottom line is that forming a group of friends who get together regularly can be done fairly easily and can have a lot of benefits. The easiest way to go about it is to start small and to get one or two other people on board who are enthusiastic. You can base it around an activity or around just hanging out.

I have found that going out with a group—whether it's to talk among ourselves or to rock the house at a party we are crashing—is totally empowering. Why should all the feeling of strength in numbers be left to gangs and fraternity brothers?

GOOD HABITS

On his deathbed some famous guy was asked if he had any regrets about his life, and he replied, "I wish I had taken better care of my teeth." I was probably in college when I heard that story. At the time, I thought it was very witty and if that was his main regret, the guy must have lived a great life. It never crossed my mind that it might be a good idea to start flossing.

It may seem very obvious to you that certain things are good for you and you should do them regularly. Maybe you have "good habits" but, in my experience, there is a huge difference between knowing that you should do certain things and actually doing them regularly.

It may seem boring, but to pick up and stick with a few good habits when you are not feeling great can actually do you a world of good—both because you feel good about yourself for being so virtuous and also because the things themselves are good for you. While the only habit that I picked up in the wake of a breakup was smoking, you need not be as stupid. Samantha, wisely, has taken another route, and I recommend that you try following her example.

After her breakup, Samantha realized that she had been essentially sleep deprived for fifteen years and that it might not hurt to try to get more sleep. She created a schedule that gave her roughly seven to eight hours of sleep every night at about the same time. And, with a few exceptions here and there, she stuck to it. After a few months, Samantha said that she was able to fall asleep more easily and sleep through the night better. Most important, she felt a lot better—she had more energy, was less moody, and didn't get sick as often. She looked much better too.

Maybe sleeping more or better isn't your thing. But the point is that it's as good a time as any to try to incorporate some behavioral changes into your life. They don't need to be gigantic or even very time-consuming. Along with flossing, pick one or two from the following list and give them a shot: wash your face before bed, exercise three times a week, drink three glasses of water a day, use eye cream, wear sun-block every day, stretch in the morning, take calcium. I'm not expecting that these things alone are going to make you feel fantastic, but every little good thing that you do for yourself helps now and later.

WHEREVER YOU ARE

Wherever you live, it's probably a far more interesting place than you realize or that you take advantage of. It's so easy to narrow a town or a city down to a handful of locales that you go to regularly and a few more that you check out every now and then. This is true if you live in New York City or if you live in Lubbock.

And quite possibly you and your ex went to a lot of places that are "your" places so they may not feel as "yours" right now. Or they may have a lot of fresh memories attached to them. Maybe you are avoiding your regular hangouts or maybe you are going to them anyway. The point is, why not take this opportunity to bust out a little?

It's possible that you end up trapped in your chair at a horrible performance art show for several hours. It's also possible that you end up finding the most kick-ass salsa dancing place or the best old movie theater or a hotel with a pool you can sneak into on hot days. Or you find a beautiful building you'd like to sketch or a park you never knew existed or a new place to watch the sun set.

Wherever you live—even if you don't love it—it's where you are now. Why not get to know it better and make more of it yours for the time that you are there? Check out your local newspaper or a Web site like www.citysearch.com, and make a point of going someplace you've never been before once a month.

THE OBVIOUS

Emily offered to smack me if I included ideas like going to museums and taking classes in this book, so it's at some risk that I'm doing it anyway. Emily lives in a place where there are many famous museums and many schools and it's clearly been suggested to her too many times that she check them out as interesting new activities in the wake of a breakup or just as a single woman in general. But no matter how many annoying people suggest it to you (including me), taking a class or making museum-going a more regular part of your life when coming out of a big change like a breakup—or at anytime—is a rock-solid way to spend free time.

First of all, I wouldn't exist if it weren't for museums. My parents met while they were taking in an exhibit separately on their lunch hours. Just as he was leaving, my father spotted my mother and approached her. He suavely asked her if she was Bolivian. She is not—she is French—but somehow this unusual opening line led to living together, marriage, and me and my brother. I'm not suggesting you go to museums to meet men or that you get involved with men who ask you strange questions, but museums are cool. So are historical societies, landmarks, libraries, zoos, and aquariums.

And I think that classes, though sometimes pricey, are the best. They can make you feel purposeful and engaged in life and productive. They bring you in contact with new ideas and new people who share at least one of your interests. And the best part is that when you aren't in school officially, who cares about grades or even perfect attendance? Plus, you don't have to take a hard class or a class related to your job or a class with homework to reap the general benefits. In fact, I think it's a great idea to take a class in something that has nothing to do with the other parts of your life as it is right now. Basket weaving, Thai cooking, belly dancing, tarot card reading, watercoloring, wine tasting—the possibilities are endless.

Finally, many many painters, musicians, writers, actors have turned heartbreak into great works of art. Why not you? No pressure, of course, and maybe artistic self-expression isn't for you, but it can't hurt to try your hand at something artistic. You can always destroy it later if you want to.

VOLUNTEERING

You may not be feeling fantastic about yourself right now, but there are people and causes all around you that could use your help. You may not feel that you have much to give, but that's not true. If you can read this book, for example, you can very likely teach someone else how to read, or help a kid with his homework, or read aloud to someone who has lost her vision. And that's just for starters.

You may not be inclined to spend your free time volunteering; maybe you spend too much of your time already helping people. Maybe volunteering seems too overwhelming and emotionally draining. But there are so many millions of ways— big, small, intense, mellow, time-consuming and not—to do good. And it may pull you out of your own problems a bit to be part of the solution to others' problems or to do something to contribute to social or environmental causes that you believe in. Start small. Take a bag of clothes to the Salvation Army near you. See how it makes you feel. At the very least, you've made some headway decluttering your closet. (For info on volunteering opportunities, check out *www.volunteermatch.com* or contact a local community center or religious organization.)

CONCLUSION

If you have made it through months two and three, you are on your way out of heartbreak hotel. You may still feel fragile sometimes. You may not be ready to throw a big party in your honor, but you deserve one. So don't uncork the bubbly. But do something to mark your progress. It may be time for dancing even if it's just you and/or some friends at home. Or maybe it's time to get out of town for the weekend on a mini–road trip or time to go visit someone you love whom you haven't seen in a while.

You may not feel like you are 100 percent in the clear, but you've got to admit that you are, on the whole, feeling a hell of a lot better than you did a month or two months ago. Take some pride in your strength. You may have discovered that you have more of it than you realized. The challenge ahead is to continue healing and turning some of that strength into making your life better than ever.

Top 5 Albums for Dancing Fools

1. **Jamiroquai**—*Traveling Without Moving*: If this doesn't get you sashaying around your pad, nothing will. "Virtual

Reality" is so jamming that it may be unsafe to listen to it while driving.

2. **Madonna**—*The Immaculate Collection*: What can I really say? You know most of these songs by heart. Madonna has achieved total world domination. It can't hurt to catch a dose of the empowerment.

3. **Tito Puente**—*Mucho Cha Cha*: The album title should make you smile, and that's only the beginning. I find that I do most of my best cha-cha-ing alone as there are fewer feet to step on. Su casa es Tito's casa.

4. **Millenium Disco Party**—*The Divas*: This is a no-brainer. Disco is about one thing and one thing only: boogying on down. With this album cranking, you will not be able to resist the groove.

5. **B-52s**—*Cosmic Thing*: Love shack, baby. That's exactly what your house will feel like when you have this album playing. This album also goes well with go-go boots, heavy eyeliner, and a teased hairdo.

Top 5 Moisturizers

1. **Clinique's Dramatically Different**: I could not have made it through high school without this one. It's perfect for combination skin.

2. **Oil of Olay Protective Renewal Lotion**: You can get it at any drugstore and it comes in an attractive bottle.

3. **Clarins Gentle Day Cream**: I started using this one when the makeup artist on a movie pointed out that my skin was a travesty. It's a little expensive, but I figure that she knows more than most mortals about skin care, and her advice—if

I'd been paying for it—would have set me back more than 100 jars of the cream.

4. **Roc Long Lasting Facial Moisturizer**: Again, this comes in a groovy bottle, is available at the drugstore, and Holly's fancy dermatologist swears by it.

5. **Kiehl's**: When in doubt, just call 1-800-KIEHLS-1 and tell them what is up with your face. Their products aren't the cheapest, but they are worth it.

Top 5 Celebrity Breakups

Here's the deal. Your breakup sucked and you and your ex may have a lot of mutual friends who heard all about it. But at least you didn't have to go through your breakup with the entire world—literally—watching.

1. **Minnie Driver and Matt Damon**: At least you didn't find out that you and your boyfriend were broken up by hearing him announce it on *Oprah*. That's never good. It's also not easy to have to attend the Oscars a few months later and act gracious when your ex is there with his new girlfriend, Winona Ryder, and also wins an award.

2. **Phil Collins and his Ex-Wife**: It is my understanding that the former Mrs. Collins, who had been married to Phil for years—not months—found out that they were getting divorced via fax. Yeah, Phil couldn't be bothered to deliver the news in person so he chose the next best way—faxing. What a jerk.

3. **Sylvester Stallone and Jennifer Flavin**: I know that they are now together and totally in love and happy and have one

or several beautiful children. But only a few short years ago, when Sly decided that he wanted out, he chose the most sensitive and thoughtful way that he could to break the news. He sent Jennifer a note via FedEx. What is that?

4. **Emma Thompson and Kenneth Branagh**: So Kenneth goes on location to direct a movie and starts having a very public affair with his leading lady, Helena Bonham-Carter. Did he think that his wife, Emma Thompson, wasn't going to find out when a million reporters were immediately calling her to get her reaction? Or maybe he thought she wouldn't care. It just makes me glad that his career seems to be tanking while Emma just keeps on rocking.

5. **Princess Di and Prince Charles**: I'm sorry, but did he say tampon? If you've been living under a rock you may have missed the private telephone conversations between Camilla Parker Bowles and Prince Charles that became extremely public. Admittedly, His Royal Tampon did not know his phone was being tapped, but come on.

Top 5 Books to Amuse and Improve

1. *Date Like a Man: What Men Know About Dating and Are Afraid You'll Find Out* by Myreah Moore and Jodie Gould: This book comes highly recommend by Lucy, who said it was not only totally hysterical but also really useful in the choppy waters of dating.

2. *Bad Girl's Guide to the Open Road* by Cameron Tuttle: If you are ready to ditch everything and head for the open road, or even if you don't have a license, this book will crack you up with indispensable information, like eleven uses for a condom besides sex.

3. ***Real Gorgeous: The Truth About Body and Beauty*** by Kaz Cooke: Cooke takes on the diet, beauty, and fashion industries' definition of beauty in this warm and humorous book that can help any woman make friends with her body. Emily especially likes the cartoons.

4. ***Three Black Skirts: All You Need to Survive*** by Anna Johnson: This book manages to be very broad in scope and yet totally cohesive and delightful. From how to fix your sink to how to cultivate your own personal style to how to protect the environment, the tone is joyous and the advice solid.

5. ***Kiss My Tiara: How to Rule the World as a Smartmouth Goddess*** by Susan Jane Gillman: Gillman's bad-ass grandmother provides a lot of the hilarity in this very funny book about issues women face today. I found the idea that if you have trouble ordering a dessert, you're going to have trouble asking for a raise both amusing and intriguing.

Top 5 On-Line Dating Services

It seems that with the hectic pace of people's lives, on-line dating has become one of the most popular ways for people to meet. About half of the single women I know have gone on dates with people they met on-line, and I know three married couples who met on-line. It may not be for you, but it's fun to check out either way. On most sites, you can look at member profiles for free but you have to sign up in order to get member contact information. Wherever you live, you can probably find some members who live not too far from you. And if you want to stay anonymous at first, you can just list your name as "Jane Doe" or whatever name you like. Here are sites that seem to have the most members and/or that my girlfriends have used.

1. www.nerve.com
2. www.match.com
3. www.matchnet.com. This site owns several dating related sites including international personals: www.americansingles.com, www.jdate.com (Jewish singles), and www.social-net.com.
4. www.drip.com. It's only in the northeast, but they actually set up dates.
5. www.matchmaker.com

QUIZ #4
Do You Have a Grip?

It's been three months or so and it's a good idea to consider whether you have a firm grasp on the reality of the breakup. Also, you want to make sure that you are taking that reality and moving in the right direction with it.

Do you blame yourself for the breakup?
If the answer is NO: You need to go out and get yourself a nice bottle of wine or a beautiful candle or do something that floats your boat. It is so common and so easy to get rutted in blaming yourself that if you are not, you really should congratulate yourself.
If the answer is YES: You are in good company, but it's time to really work this through. Revisit the sections on blaming yourself and blaming your ex and write out all your feelings on the blame topic. Also, ask a compassionate friend to talk through your feelings of responsibility with you. If you still feel that you are trapped in the blame zone, get professional help. Feelings of blame are a natural part of the recovery process, but you can't keep healing if you can't get past them.

Can you say that you are single without bursting into tears?
If the answer is NO: If you burst into tears every time the word *single* even crosses your mind, you need to step back to the beginning of Chapter 3. You also might want to get some help.

Acceptance of the way your life is right now is important so that you can work from there to make it better. If you burst into tears on the single topic only infrequently, you are on the right track. A few more weeks and you will probably not shed a tear at all.

If the answer is YES: All right, you dry-eyed mama! Probably your lack of tears indicates that you are doing pretty well and that you are fairly comfortable accepting what has happened. However, if you never ever cry—not even while watching *Beaches*—you may have supersonic powers of repression and denial, and should probably reach out for assistance from a pro.

Have you been acting out your revenge fantasies?

If the answer is NO: Good, then you are not reading this from behind bars. Nice going.

If the answer is YES: Is this book in prison libraries? Let me know. If your acting out has not led to any kind of interaction with the fuzz, consider yourself lucky and put your revenge days behind you and make "living well is the best revenge" your mantra.

Have you had anyone over to your home since the breakup?

If the answer is NO: That's what I call very not good. Grab the phone and rustle up a few friends for dinner at your casa next week. Tidy up a touch if necessary, and if cooking or even warming TV dinners is too much, make it potluck or order in.

If the answer is YES: If the only time people have been over is the first week of the breakup to bring you Kleenex and beer, that doesn't count. I'm not talking about having people over to check whether you are all right, I'm talking having people over for an evening of your great company and to check up on you very subtly. If you have had people over and you behaved like a seminormal hostess, you rule.

Have you had a night out with your girlfriends since the breakup?

If the answer is NO: Your answer begs the question of whether you have been out at all since the breakup because who are you going to go out with when you are feeling so-so besides your girlfriends? You have either got to accept the next mellow invitation to go out with your friends, or you need to call some of them now and make a plan to gather.

If the answer is YES: If you have been out with one girlfriend to an empty bar in the middle of the day and you spent the whole time crying, then you and I are not talking about the same thing. If you have spent an evening out that was considered enjoyable to you *and* your girlfriends, then we are speaking the same language and you are fighting back nicely.

Have you tried to incorporate a new good habit into your life?

If the answer is NO: I can't force you, but I recommend that you give it a shot ASAP. If you don't floss, just try it once. It's disgusting in there. How can you choose not to once you've seen—dare I say smelled—what happens between your pearly whites without it?

If the answer is YES: Jump back and kiss yourself. Keep it up!

I guess it comes down to this: If you are still crying often and can't bring yourself to do anything social or good for yourself, you are still on shaky ground. You may want to glance back at Chapter 3 before moving ahead and see if anything sinks in better now. You may also want to get some extra support now or soon. If you are feeling better and feel as if you are on track with most of the questions, congratulate yourself and read on.

4. three to six months:
BACK TO LIFE

Quite possibly you've started noticing the world around you again—the pretty flowers, the smell of trash, the hot guy on the subway. You are coming back to life. You may feel as if you are surfacing for air after being submerged in water for a long time. You may feel a jolt of amazement at each little thing that makes you smile. The pain that you thought might never go away has greatly diminished or actually stopped.

Now what? It's possible that—with the exception of your recent breakup—you are content with your life and yourself the way it and you are right now. And you may also feel that not crying every night is its own reward. But is that really enough? You obviously have a great amount of strength and resilience—more than you may have even realized before the breakup. What if you took some of it and applied it to growing in addition to healing?

part one: LIFE'S UNPREDICTABLE MOMENTS

It's possible you may not have heard or seen the very last of your ex. Even if you have been and continue to be the poster child for self-control, that unfortunately doesn't mean you can control everything. But the unexpected doesn't have to turn into the disastrous, especially when you've put a little thought into it in advance.

RANDOM PHONE CALL

It is very likely that, if it hasn't already happened, you will hear at some point from your ex. It's a rare man who wouldn't want to check in with you down the road. It may be because he's had some more experience and wonders if he made a mistake breaking up with you. It may be because he just ran across your number and wanted to say hi. Usually you get the random call just after you've finally stopped praying that it would be your ex calling every time the phone rings.

On the receiving end of that call, it can often be hard to figure out why your ex is getting in touch with you. In my experience, men making the "random call" have very little to say, making the conversation extra-awkward. But here's the thing: Even though you are a very gracious and tactful person, why make it any easier on him? He's been a complete ass or at least broke your heart. So if you get a random call from your ex and he is acting like it's perfectly normal that he should ring you up, just ask him point-blank, "Why are you calling?" Let him squirm. You've squirmed plenty trying to figure out what went wrong and how to get your life together again. If your ex mumbles some feeble answer like he was just calling to say hi and see how you were, be strong. You may in your heart still want to stay on the phone with him forever, but remember that your ex has no business calling you casually. If he's calling to talk seriously or to apologize, that's one thing. But if he's not, you should tell him that under the circumstances you think it's best he didn't call you. You can do it. It totally sucks, of course, but do not let your ex draw you back into a situation where you don't know where you stand, or where your fragile mind is going to start rehashing everything and wondering if he's going to call again and if you two are getting back together. It may not seem like much, but right now you've gotten to a place where at least you know that the relationship is over and you've done a lot of the hard-core grieving. Don't let your ex tamper with your progress unless he's got something major to say. Finally, don't second-guess yourself. If your ex has something that he really really wants to say and you cut him short, he'll call you back.

SURPRISE RUN-INS

It's not a pleasant thought, but it's probably already crossed your mind, and if you and your ex still live in the same town, it could well happen. I once had the devastating experience of running into an ex of mine (whom I was still heartbroken over) not once but twice in the same evening. He was with two women, one of whom he'd already slept with and the other I later found out he was sleeping with at the time. What those two women were thinking I don't know, but I do know how wretched the experience made me feel. And twice? Just as I was crying in my beer over the first run-in, my ex and his entourage strode into the bar and sat at the table across from mine. Anyway, the good news is that the chances of this happening to you are slim. There is no bad news but I do have a few suggestions.

✿ Never approach your ex first. If he wants to come over to you, that's life. But do not go running over to him, as I have on several occasions. It's depressing and undignified and makes you feel like a loser then and later. It's hard to remember something this basic when you are taken unawares, but etch it in your mind now before any possible run-in.

✿ If you bump into your ex, and I mean literally, do not freeze and do not run. Remember that even if you think he can hear your heart thumping, he can't. Keep it short but polite and then move on to wherever you were heading, even if it was only the bathroom. If he wants to come over and chat with you later, he can.

✿ Say as little as possible. I am a blabbermouth, which has proved to be really unfortunate in surprise run-ins. It becomes a little like an out-of-body experience and I see myself blathering away like an idiot and am horrified but can't stop myself. In advance of a possible surprise encounter, think of Lauren Bacall. LB, LB. Cool as an ice cube in the desert. She wouldn't say one darn thing more than she had to under any circumstances even if you were torturing her. Not a peep. She is the surprise run-in goddess. Try to remember her in your time of need.

✿ If you end up throwing something at your ex, it's better if it's plastic or tin like a half-empty can of Budweiser. Never throw glass or furniture. Avoiding assault charges is key.

BEING FRIENDS

A lot of people think that being able to stay friends with your exes is a sign of maturity. I don't. Staying friends with exes can be desirable, but *not* staying friends with exes can be equally desirable. The most important thing about deciding whether to be friends with your ex is waiting until you feel over him. Be honest. If you are interested in staying friends with your ex in case he changes his mind about the breakup, banish the idea of being friends from your thoughts. And if your ex wants to stay friends, never use that as an opportunity to show him how cool you can be and how fabulous you are. You are incredible whether or not your ex realizes it, and trying to prove it to him will only make you feel depressed and frustrated. And it's bad for your self-esteem. Before even contemplating staying friends with your ex, I recommend letting at least six months pass after the breakup and even possibly waiting until you are involved—and happily—with someone else. Lucy recommends waiting one year because she feels it takes that long to get a safe distance from the physical and emotional familiarity you and your ex once shared.

If a significant amount of time has passed and you are still thinking about possibly staying friends with your ex, you should consider the following:

❀ Is he a good friend to his other friends?
❀ The breakup aside, was he a good friend to you when you were going out?
❀ If you were meeting him for the first time, would your ex be the kind of person you would like to be just friends with?

A lot of people, it seems to me, stay friends with their exes because they are afraid to lose contact with people who were once so close to them. Maybe they have already lost close friends or family members and it's too painful to really let go. This may be how you feel. Just be sure that if you do end up staying friends with your ex, you leave enough room in your heart and your life for someone else to fully occupy the romantic position that your ex left open. The next man won't want to share that spot with anyone else.

part two: NO DRESS REHEARSAL

Think about your life. Isn't there room for improvement or adventure or new experiences? The freedom that comes with being single can be potentially frightening if you don't know what to do with it. But it's exciting too. You are the only person responsible for your happiness, which is fine because you are the right person for the job. I started to head this way in the "vision of life" section earlier, but let's go deeper in exploring who you are and what you want that doesn't immediately involve having a man in your life.

WHAT DO YOU WANT?

I recommend answering in writing or at least thinking about the following questions. I hope they will remind you of things that you were thinking about doing before you got sideswiped by heartbreak. Maybe they will even bring to light some things that you'd forgotten you'd ever been interested in, or maybe some new interests will emerge.

1. When you were little, what did you want to be when you grew up?
2. Are there any elements of those dreams that are part of your life today?
3. List ten things besides work that you like to do. When was the last time you did each activity?

4. List ten other things that you'd like to try.
5. Why haven't you tried some of them?

As many people get older, they feel that life narrows, and in some ways it does. For example, if you are over eighteen and you haven't been out on the ice since you were six, it's unlikely that you are going to be an Olympic skater. But does that mean you shouldn't skate? That there isn't a lot of room for achievement and satisfaction waiting for you at your nearest rink? Too many people let things they love fall away just because they think they can't make it a career. They decide it isn't worth the time and effort because it will "never go anywhere." Often they decide it can't go anywhere when that's not even necessarily true.

Lucy

Lucy has always loved making jewelry. She used to doodle necklaces and rings on every scrap of paper that came her way. She even took welding lessons in college and was really good at it. But somewhere along the line, Lucy decided that being a lawyer made more sense. She went to law school and practiced law for several years, but at some point she decided to take a jewelry design class at night to see if she still had an interest in it. She loved it and took another class and then another. A year or so after she started her first class, she ran into a classmate from high school who, it turned out, had become a jewelry buyer for an important department store. Lucy showed her old classmate some of her designs and got her first order for a few pieces. To Lucy's surprise, her pieces sold well and she got more orders. And then a few more orders. Shortly thereafter that Lucy left her law firm. Today, she has a modest jewelry business. It's not always easy going, but Lucy is happier than any of us have ever seen her. She doesn't have as lavish a lifestyle as she did as a lawyer, but she says that she never dreads getting out of bed in the morning the way she used to.

Samantha

Samantha fell in love with yoga when she was getting her master's in education to become a preschool teacher. She loved how her yoga classes made her feel after a long day assistant-teaching three-year-olds. After finishing school, Samantha got a job teaching her own classroom. She continued to go to yoga in the evenings because it made her relax and helped her stay calm with her students. One summer, Samantha decided to use her free time to do a yoga instructor program. She became certified and, in the fall, when she went back to school, she decided to use some of things she'd learned in her classroom. The kids loved it and some of the other teachers became interested. Today, in addition to teaching her regular classes, Samantha runs a "kid yoga" after-school program and has weekend classes for teachers and parents. She's delighted that she's been able to share the benefits of yoga with others and that she has combined her interest in teaching with her love of yoga. She is also happy to have a little extra income to further her own yoga studies and plans to attend a seminar in India.

Josie

Josie has always had an interest in tap dancing. She took some lessons as a girl, but her parents couldn't really afford them and after a while she stopped. Not long ago, Josie was watching an old movie with Ginger Rogers and realized that she still wanted to tap dance. She got some shoes and signed up for a class at the Y. Josie isn't planning on quitting her day job, but she feels like she's learning new things and is proud of her improvement. She doesn't expect to make it to Broadway and doesn't care whether people think tap dancing is a wacky hobby. She is really happy with it, and I bet she's the best tap-dancing marine biologist in the whole world.

Why not make an agreement with yourself to try some new things, to get around to doing more of the things you like to do, and to consider what ways you might incorporate some of your childhood dreams into your current life? You may even want to write out this agreement with yourself and date it and post it somewhere where you can see it regularly. Write out a calendar of the year and select one thing that interests you and make sure to do it within that month.

BE YOUR OWN SHRINK

This exercise is obviously not a substitute for good professional help nor is it intended to replicate that experience. But it can't hurt to ask yourself some of the questions that a professional might ask you if you walked into his or her office right now, and to answer them in writing on your own. Maybe you've already thought about these questions a lot or addressed some of them in therapy. Either way, this exercise is free, and writing down your thoughts, even if the thoughts themselves are sometimes unpleasant, can do you no harm. Be sure, after you answer each question, to sit back and ask yourself: How did [or does] this make me feel? This is perhaps the most obvious sign that you are self-shrinking correctly *and* it's the most valuable part of the process.

Get out your calendar and then book one, maybe two, fifty-minute appointments with yourself weekly for the next four weeks. Then get yourself an alarm or kitchen timer and set it for exactly fifty minutes before you start every session. Never exceed the fifty minutes; it's just not professional.

At the beginning of each session, consider outsmarting, shocking, and being dishonest with yourself. Get over it and do a check-in with yourself on anything out of the ordinary in the areas of sleep, diet, mood, exercise, and dreams. Then address the following questions where you last left off, occasionally interjecting, "That must have been difficult for you."

1. To the best of your knowledge, what were your parents' childhoods like? How would you describe your parents' relationships with their own parents?
2. What was the relationship between your parents like? Did they benefit equally from their relationship?
3. What were the other key adult relationships in your world as a child (i.e., between your mother and your stepfather)? What were they like?
4. How would you describe your relationship with your mother when you were a child?
5. How would you describe your relationship with your father when you were a child?
6. If you have a sibling or siblings, what was your relationship with him/her/them as children?
7. If you have a sibling or siblings, what were his/her/their relationship(s) with your mother and father as a child or as children?

8. How would you describe the atmosphere in your home as a child?

9. What role, if any, did alcohol or drugs play in your childhood home?

10. Were any of the relationships in your childhood home abusive—physically, emotionally, or sexually? If so, describe them.

11. Were there were any traumatic events in your childhood? If so, describe them.

12. What role, if any, did religion, race, and ethnicity play in your childhood home?

13. Were there were any health-related issues or illnesses in your childhood? If so, describe them.

14. If it hasn't already come up, did you suffer the loss of a parent or person close to you as a child or since?

15. How would you characterize your mother's (or the principal woman in your childhood's) attitude about men, sex, appearance, food, body image? How would you assess her self-esteem?

16. How would you characterize your father's (or the principal man in your childhood's) attitude about women, sex, appearance, food, body image? How would you assess his self-esteem?

17. How did you feel about school? What were your relationships like with peers and teachers?

18. Did you get into trouble as a child or teenager? If so, what kind and how did those experiences play out with the adults in your life?

19. How did you feel about leaving home? If you haven't left home, how do you feel about that?

20. How do you cope with stress/depression/anxiety?

21. How would you characterize your attitude about men, sex, appearance, food, and body image? How would you assess your own self-esteem?

22. What role, if any, do alcohol and drugs play in your life currently?

23. What is your relationship with your parents like these days? With your sibling(s)?

24. How do you feel about your current work situation or lack of work?

25. How would you characterize your relationships with friends and colleagues?

26. How would you characterize your relationships with men? With women?

27. What are your biggest fears?

28. What in your life makes you happy? What are the things that you are the proudest of?

29. What are your goals—professionally and personally?

If you are wondering what this exercise was supposed to do for you because you are not sure it was very helpful, I have two thoughts: (1) You may make a very good therapist; and (2) the benefits of honestly answering the questions may take some time to surface.

For me, thinking about these questions was a really important step in figuring out who I am and taking responsibility for my life. Figuring out what was painful and what was joyful about my childhood, what my parents were like as parents and as people—among other issues—enabled me to be a more compassionate person to myself and with others. It also helped me hone in on three topics: fear, forgiveness, and gratitude. Without exploring these questions, I'm not sure I would have come to understand why and how much fear had come to influence my decision making, how forgiveness of myself and others could help me assuage my fears and help me move ahead with my life, and how gratitude could center me in the face of every-day annoyances as well as in more serious turmoil.

It seems to me that every adult should be able to answer the above questions if only to get clear on who he or she is. Even if answering them isn't rocking your world, you have done a lot more than most in getting to know yourself. And, in the best-case scenario, the information that you have brought to light can help you avoid re-creating some things that you didn't like about your early life and help you embrace the things you did. It can help you move beyond unhealthy and potentially cyclical patterns of behavior of your own or of your immediate family. I suppose that the bottom line is that if you can strike a balance of forgiveness and responsibility in your past and integrate that into the person that you are, you stand a far greater chance of withstanding the challenges that life presents and receiving the blessings, big and small, that the world holds in store for you.

Any which way, if you actually complete this exercise, though I said it was free, I think you should pay yourself. Depending on your health insurance or lack thereof, each of these appointments might have cost you between $5 and $200, and you should spend whatever you think would be appropriate on yourself right now. Remember that even useless sessions in therapy have to be paid for.

SOLITUDE

Unlike loneliness, which I talked about earlier, solitude is a chosen state—the experience of spending time alone by choice. It seems to me that women more than men are encouraged from the time that we are small to be constantly social and to be part of groups. Perhaps this was initially intended to keep us safe from marauding tribes or outlaws. I don't know, but I think that women are less likely to be encouraged to cultivate an enjoyment of spending time alone or pursuing solitary activities. As a result, many of us are not that comfortable being alone—even if we spend a lot of time alone. We associate being alone with retreating in depression, anger, sickness, or grief because those are the rare times we have actually chosen to be alone. We often think of the state of being alone as lonely. That need not be the case.

Solitude is as important as socializing. It is time to quiet the mind, let new ideas percolate, and digest the experience of being with others. It's time when you can get back in touch with the private essential you. And it's a little harder and less obvious than it sounds.

In order to experience solitude, you clearly need to be alone, but it's not as simple as being alone. You can't be paying bills, worrying about who is or isn't calling, or feeling pressure to be productive. You don't have to stare at the wall and do nothing (though that's fine too), but you can't do anything that's an obligation or feels like a drag. Solitude isn't about an activity, though you can experience solitude while doing certain activities you like but that don't involve a lot of active thinking. Listening to an old jazz album or repotting a plant works for me as do activities that involve a lot of repetition like chopping vegetables or swimming laps.

You may already be a master of solitude, in which case I high-five you. I am not, but I'm getting better. In the past, when I was alone—by choice or not—I would always "keep busy" or get on the phone. And internally, my brain was always fairly frantic with minutiae like: Do I need to get that last wisdom tooth out? Did I forget to call my aunt on her birthday? Is Miller Lite better than Amstel Light? What is the interest rate on my Visa card? Why do I never have any pants I like? Did I ever use that $10 credit at Macy's? How many wedding presents do I still need to get? Can I afford them? Recently, I have started spending time alone better. I've stopped trying to distract myself, and I have found that after a while I'm able to get my brain to shut up.

If you find that you are constantly distracting yourself with busywork and frantic thoughts when you are alone, you too may not be that good at solitude. But experiencing and learning to enjoy solitude is so important for your mental health, and for a fuller appreciation of yourself and life, that I suggest you try the following.

Make a date to spend half an hour with yourself alone. Turn off the TV, the phone ringer, the answering machine, the radio. Give yourself something really easy to do during that time. At first, you may find that many thoughts are whizzing through your mind, including self-critical ones like, "This is just an excuse to be lazy" or "I don't meet enough new men and this isn't helping" or "This is boring" or "I should be exercising right now." Let your thoughts flow through you but don't act on them. You may not find that your thoughts slow down during your first "solitude date." Make another date with yourself and make it a little longer. Keep going until you find that you are able to be alone without distractions or frantic thinking.

PRIVATE RITUALS

Samantha mentioned to me last year that Rene Russo prays a lot. She knows this because one of her yoga teachers is Rene

Russo's stand-in and Rene told her. Then Emily, who considers herself an atheist, told me that if she ever got sick she would ask people to pray for her. She said that in her work in hospitals it seems that patients who have people praying for them just do better. Now it's not like these were the first two times I'd heard of praying and the power of prayer, but for some reason something clicked for me and I thought: Why not pray?

I wasn't taught to pray and I didn't grow up in a religious home, so at first I wasn't sure how to go about it. Getting on your knees and clasping your hands together seemed like an obvious place to start. At first it made me a little nervous to just improvise with the actual prayer, but I'm over that now. It feels healthy for me to take some time at the end of my day to send love to people in my life and people in the world at large who have come to my attention. I like the idea that my voice joins a vast chorus of people sending love out of themselves to others. It also gives me a moment to be grateful for what I have and to put whatever challenges I'm facing into context. Finally, even though at this point I have no idea to whom or what I'm praying beyond the universe and the spirits of the people I've loved who are now dead, it just feels good to ask for help, for some extra strength. I can't say whether my praying has changed my life or the lives of the people I'm praying for. Who knows? I feel good about it and that's enough.

Now, praying may not be for you. Even so, I think it's a good idea to create some private rituals, small and simple ceremonies that you can do often and anywhere that provide a little time for reflection and make you feel good. They honor you and maybe they honor others as well. Most cultures provide examples that are usually associated with religious beliefs. You don't have to include an organized religion into your life to benefit from the soothing power of rituals. A ritual that you create is as valid and powerful as any other.

If you don't already have some private rituals in your life, try incorporating one of the following: Write one page in a journal every day, light candles at home for yourself or others, read an inspirational poem aloud every night, listen to your favorite song every morning, lie on the floor for five minutes before bed and focus on your breathing.

I find that private rituals, in addition to their other benefits, are helpful in breaking away from what I call "Big Brother" syndrome. Even in the privacy of their own homes, people often continue to feel self-conscious, asking themselves, "What would so-and-so think of this?" or "I'd be embarrassed if so-and-so saw me now." It has become such a big part of our lives, in work and in social contexts, to be concerned with what other people think of us that it is very hard to turn off that inner voice even at home. Private rituals can help you develop of a feeling of real privacy in your home, as in your mind. They can help you turn off or tone down your self-conscious voice. And they provide an excellent opportunity for you to cultivate a feeling of not caring what at least your ex in particular would think about anything that you are doing.

LOVE, YOU, AND EXPECTATIONS

A lot of people think that love is the answer to all the Big Questions. Why are we here? Love. What is the meaning of life? Love. What gives our lives significance? Love. What makes us whole? Love. Love. Love. Love. And so in the wake of a breakup, people often feel that they have lost more than the love of one person—they have lost their reason for being.

But, of course, the love that is the answer to the Big Questions is not the love of one man; it's Love with a capital *L* and includes many different kinds of love. Love of self. Love of animals. Love of family. Love of friends. Love of work. Love of art. Love of fellow humans. Love of children. Love of delicious snacks. Love of bad TV. Love of anything and everything.

Yet it often seems to me that romantic love is the kind of love that most people think of when they think about Big Questions. Is it because it feels like magic? Is it because it can lead to the birth of children? Is it because it can lead to the wearing of dress that looks a little like a tutu? Is it because, in this culture, the bonds of family and religion are looser than they once were? I'm not sure. And I'm not saying that romantic love isn't mysterious, thrilling, and powerful and that it hasn't always been so. It's just that it seems a little unbalanced to expect romantic love to be Love, and it doesn't give much credit to the many kinds of love that you give and receive all the time.

I think it's a good idea, especially before you get into a new relationship, to ask yourself what you expect from romantic love. Do you expect it to make you happy? Do you expect it to jump-start you into a new career or finally losing five pounds? Do you expect it to improve your relationship with your mother? Do you expect it to make your job more interesting? Do you expect it to make you more financially secure? Do you expect it to make you feel better about yourself? Do you expect it to make your social life more interesting? What do you expect? After you've blurted out the things that you expect from romantic love—the things that pop into your mind most easily—think about those expectations again. Are they realistic?

FREEDOM, BABY

A lot of the current advice being given to women on dating and marriage harkens back to a time before many of us were even born, a time *before* it was normal for women to go to college, or have a job, or have sex with more than one person in their whole lifetime. Women are instructing women to "let your date do the talking" or "turn your finances over to your husband—it will make him feel important." I find it really unsettling.

It reminds me of an evening I spent in the company of several of my older female relatives who tag-teamed me and advised me that a man "won't buy the cow if he can get the milk for free." At first their advice made me mad. I had worked hard in school, gotten into a good college, gotten a good job. Did all that make me just a cow? And why wasn't my brother a cow too? On top of it, I was living with a boyfriend at the time. I'm not sure if you would call the milk "free," but it was flowing. It took me some time to realize that these women in my family— many of whom were born around the turn of the last century and weren't able even to vote until their late twenties, by which time they already had several children—never experienced any measure of independence from men. At an age determined by their parents, they took their youth and presumed virtue, and exchanged it for marriage, acceptable social standing, and possibly (but not always) a measure of financial security. These women could not conceive of a young woman managing in the world without the protection of a man. The huge chasm between the world they grew up in and the world I grew up in left them concerned about me, and me somewhat shocked.

As for the women giving retro advice today, they depress me. They are working women who have enjoyed many of our new freedoms but are trying to sell us on the idea that we are just cows with jobs. Instead of acknowledging that the world has changed, they are offering us advice that sounds familiar and plays on familiar fears. But that doesn't make it good or relevant to our lives. We've all heard our great-aunts, grandmothers, maybe even our mothers whispering about us at family functions, but are we really looking to re-create their experiences? I'm not saying that we don't have a lot to learn from the women who came before us but, at least in this country, things have changed a great deal and we don't have to carry around old fears or play by old rules.

Think about this: Who was the first person you ever went out with for a few months? Now imagine being married to him—for fifty years. If our mothers hadn't fought to change our world, that's very likely what would have happened to all of us. So the world has changed, and you may feel those changes led you to your more recent heartbreak in some way. You slept with and dated and maybe even lived with a man whom you aren't going to spend the rest of your life with. But you probably wouldn't have even gotten to meet your ex if things were the way they once were. Or go to a coed school. Or hold your job. Or go to a bar with your girlfriends. Or live on your own. Or decide when was the right time for you to get pregnant. Or make most of the decisions that you have made for yourself and make for yourself every day.

This is what I am saying: Embrace your freedoms, even if it means that life doesn't always turn out the way you want, because the alternatives were not and are not better. We romanticize them when we get scared, but that's not the answer. In many parts of the world, women are still fighting for rights we take for granted. They are fighting to vote, to wear pants, to drive, to leave their houses unaccompanied, to choose whom they marry, to go to school. And it wasn't that long ago that women here were fighting for those same things here. Our lives have new challenges, but we are more free than women have ever been in the history of the world.

What does that mean for you? It means that you have the chance to be whoever you want to be *and*, if you want, share your life with a man. That may not seem like a whole lot to you, but it's actually a recent and rare opportunity. Don't look backward to help you figure out how to do it. Trust yourself. Like it or not, you are making history.

THE WAITING GAME

When Josie went through her last breakup, I remember her asking me, in a sad moment, when her life was going to start. She felt as if she were waiting—waiting to get married, to buy a house, to have children. Without these things, she felt that she was still a kid waiting to grow up, on the sidelines of adult life. You may not feel this way, but I think that many women do.

It's very recent that a single woman in our culture can be in-dependent—financially and socially—from her family, that she can be a grown-up on her own. Strong, sexy, successful, and solo. And it's going to take a little while for everyone to get their minds around that, including maybe even us. We know things have changed. I mean, is Sandra Bullock an old maid? Is Cameron Diaz a spinster? But have we changed how we think of ourselves?

In the few months after Josie's breakup, her feelings about herself and her life did start to change. Josie realized that she didn't have to feel as if she was waiting for her life to start if she didn't want to and that her grown-up identity did not have to depend on being married or being a mother. She could begin treating herself like she was a grown-up immediately and she could also reasonably expect others to do the same. On her next family vacation, she declined to share a room with her ten-year-old cousin. She stayed in and paid for her own hotel room. She started renting her own cars when she went out of town to visit friends. She invited her family to have Thanksgiving at her house. And she decided to stop postponing some decisions that she had assumed she would make with a man. She got a dog. She bought a bed.

Josie still wants to get married and have a family someday, and she's not sure when that's going to happen. But in the meantime, she's realized that she can make the feeling of waiting diminish by living as if her life has already started and treating herself like a grown-up. She feels more confident and thinks that "not waiting" is going to help her meet a man who is a grown-up too.

It's a good idea to see what role, if any, "waiting" plays in your life.

✿ Do you feel like you are waiting to be married or to be a mother for your life to start? If so, why? What role does other people's view of you affect your thoughts on this topic?

✿ Are you are waiting until you have a man in your life to do certain things? If so, why?

✿ Do you feel like you are waiting to be a grown-up? If so, what changes can you make to feel like one now?

SENSE OF PURPOSE

Having a sense of purpose in life is obviously a good thing. It gives your life meaning and direction. It gives you a reason to get up in the morning. It helps you go on living in bad—even tragic—times, and it makes your life fuller in the best of times.

For many people their sense of purpose in life is related to family, however they define family. For some people family means the spouse and children they hope to have. For others it means a close circle of friends. For some people family is their parents, their siblings, nephews, nieces, cousins. And for most people what gives them a sense of purpose is the relationships they have with some combination of the people in these different versions of family. And that's normal, but I think it's equally important and healthy for you *and* for the people you love to cultivate a parallel sense of purpose that is not dependent on anyone but you.

When it comes to other people, we have limited control. You can't control when you will meet the man of your dreams or have children any more than you can control your parents, your siblings, or your friends. You can't control when people move, how they change, or how their need for you changes. You can't prevent your daughter from growing up and going away to school. You can't stop your parents from growing old. You can't prevent your best friend from getting married and moving to Hong Kong. You can't stop your teenage brother from flipping you the bird and shutting you out of his life. But you can control whether your life is meaningful to you if you cultivate a personal and independent sense of purpose.

But in addition to or besides connection to some version of family, what can provide a sense of purpose? Making the world a better place in some way. Helping others. Expressing oneself creatively. Making use of one's talents. Personal growth. Serving and practicing a religion or system of spiritual beliefs. Some combination of these. It seems that a personal sense of purpose can be related to work or might not be, and that a strong personal sense of purpose isn't something that can easily be affected by others. For example, if you can't get a record deal, it might be hard to be a rock star, but you can still make music. It also seems that your personal sense of purpose can change as you change, or as you reach new levels of accomplishment. For example, after you've achieved total enlightenment, you may want to share your passion for square dancing with children in New Zealand.

Finding or developing a sense of purpose or maintaining one in the face of life's obstacles is not easy and is, in some ways, the challenge of a lifetime, so don't freak out if you find it a daunting proposition. But it's definitely worth thinking about.

ROMANCING YOUR OWN LIFE

Romance is most often associated with romantic love. You think of a candlelit dinner for two with a view of the Eiffel Tower. Or you think of dancing cheek to cheek under the stars. And it's great to experience romance that involves two people. But romance is actually much more than a prelude to a kiss or a marriage; it's a way of life.

You may already live romantically, in which case I salute you. But it took me some time to get hip to it. At first, I thought romance was what a man was going to bring into my life. Then I realized it wasn't necessarily so. Then I had to figure out what living romantically meant to me and how to go about it. It's a work in progress, but the more romance I bring into my life, the sexier, funnier, smarter I feel.

There are many ways to bring romance into your life, but the basic tenet of living a romantic life is maximizing the enjoyment of your senses: sight, sound, smell, touch, taste. These senses don't exist just to help us understand the world outside ourselves; they exist for our own pleasure and amusement. Otherwise, cod liver oil and a fine wine would taste the same.

Some ways to romance your life include wearing lipstick at home, wearing perfume all the time, wearing suave undergarments, sleeping on silk sheets or in sassy lingerie, having flowers in your home, bathing by candlelight, skinny-dipping, listening to Barry White or opera, wearing a scarf and glasses like Grace Kelly or Jackie O., eating outdoors, using wineglasses, cooking any recipe with garlic or basil, drinking a beverage with real mint leaves in it, lying naked under a ceiling fan, taking a walk in the rain, wearing body oil, burning sage, getting or giving a massage, soaking your feet with rose petals, working up a good sweat, watching the moon rise, listening to a brook babble, sipping a brandy, growing herbs, letting a pet lick your face, sticking your head in the freezer, wearing clothes that are your favorite color or fabric, listening to a Nina Simone album in the dark.

If you feel that you need some more romance in your life, make a list of your senses and list five things under each sense that soothe or titillate. Then get busy and work on regularly incorporating more and varied sensual pleasure into your life.

THE ROLE OF LUCK IN LOVE

You may find that as soon as you are single, people will start offering their advice—usually unsolicited—about how you should go about meeting men. As I see it, the advice usually falls into two categories. There's the "get out there and find him!" approach favored by most women's magazines and perky people everywhere. And there's the "clueless" approach favored by, among others, Josie.

The "get out there and find him!" approach is fairly self-evident. Like a hunter stalking prey, you must put yourself in as many situations as possible where you will meet men. You should identify the places the kind of man you might be interested in would hang out and you should go there. Some of the more irritating proponents of this approach toss in extra advice for when you are in the right company, like "act like a klutz" or "stare at him and then walk away" and other such gems.

Pros:

It's good to go to new places. It's good to meet new people. It's good to meet men if you are looking to meet a man.

Cons:

It's exhausting. How many nights a week can you devote, or do you want to devote, to looking your best *and* being coy?

The "clueless" approach means that the less you think about finding true love—that is, the more "clueless" you are to wanting to be with someone—the more likely you are to find it/him. There is not much to this approach except squelching any anxiety you might have about ever meeting someone and just going about your business as usual.

Pros:

It's not taxing. You're not changing your routine.

Cons:

If you are a homebody and don't make more of an effort to meet people, it's unlikely that you are going to meet many new men.

The thing that always amazes me about people who strongly advocate either of these approaches is that they seem to think that an "approach" will help you find love. They seem to be forgetting the important role that luck plays in meeting the right person.

Finding love isn't a numbers game. You can "get out there!" and meet tons of men but not meet someone who is right for you. Or you might be at a singles' event one night and meet your perfect match. Or you can be in the Laundromat thinking about whites versus colors and meet someone terrific.

Finding love isn't about attitude, either. You can meet the right person for you when you are looking for love *or* you can find love when you aren't looking for it.

Many of us have been taught to work hard or have a mental strategy for the things we want—in work or in school. For better or worse, love isn't like that. You might find love by being ferocious about Internet dating or you might find love in the lobby of your building coming in from a rainstorm.

I recommend that you make some effort to meet new people but don't drive yourself crazy with it. And don't let other people make you feel bad about not "getting out there" as much as they think you should. When it comes to love, the two best things that you can do have little to do with actually meeting people. They have to do with you: making your life full and interesting to you and making sure that you are the best you can be emotionally.

CONCLUSION

You've made it! You have lived through the first six months following the breakup, and you are going to be just fine. You may already be feeling that you are going to be better than ever. You may not. But either way, you are a different person than you were six short months ago. Because as horribly painful as this breakup was and may still feel at times, you have grown.

I hope that you have learned as much as you can from the relationship and the breakup. Mostly, I hope that you have learned a lot about yourself—about how strong you are, how smart, how beautiful, how funny, and how deserving of a rare love. You clearly were and are capable of loving powerfully and of suffering powerfully. That kind of passion and caring is a sign of a rich and courageous heart and mind. I hope that you will put your heart and mind to their best use—making your own life full and continuing to share yourself with others as truly as you can.

Top 5 Books Every Woman Should Own

All right, I admit that this list is a little heavy. But empowerment isn't always easy and these books are worth the effort.

1. *Our Bodies, Ourselves: A Book by and for Women* by the Boston Women's Health Book Collective: This book was originally written in the 1960s and was one of the most important books of that era. It may not seem that radical today, but it was the first book to ever provide comprehensive information about the unique health and emotional issues that women face written with love by women. It's been updated recently to keep up with new attitudes and advances in medicine and continues to be the best general look at the experience of being a woman and living in a woman's body.

2. *And Still I Rise:* Poetry by Maya Angelou: These poems are beautiful and inspirational. They speak to the experience of being a woman of any time, of any color, of any place. The book includes a poem called "Phenomenal Woman," and being one yourself, you should check it out.

3. *The Artist's Way* by Julia Cameron: This book is good for everyone who wants to make the most of herself. You don't have to want to be an artist or writer or painter to use this book to further discover yourself, build your confidence, and get closer to achieving your goals, whatever they are.

4. *Live in a Better Way: Reflections on Truth, Love and Happiness* by the Dalai Lama: This totally understandable book is not about religion or Buddhism per se. It's a short collection of four lectures that the Dalai Lama gave, and it's really about how to better understand yourself and others, how to deal with negative feelings, and how to live a decent life that honors yourself and others. The world would be a better place if everyone read this book and took just one of these ideas into his or her heart.

5. *The Feminine Mystique* by Betty Friedan: Have you heard of Martin Luther King, Jr.? Have you heard of Malcolm X? They are heroes who made incredible contributions to civil rights in this country and life as we know it here. So too is Betty Friedan a hero. The women's rights movement that changed our world forever and for the better is less than forty years old, and yet so many of us know so little about it. Freedoms we take for granted were hard won by women like Betty Friedan, and I think that every woman in this country should be familiar with this important work. The sections on homosexuality are dated and totally off, but it is still a critical read.

Top 5 Marriage Myths

You may be wondering what these are doing in this book. There are actually two reasons: (1) I think if I and some of my friends had been clued into these earlier and given them some thought, we might have made more of ourselves and our lives when we were single; and (2) I think marriage is held out in our culture as the Answer, and that creates unrealistic and inflated expectations.

1. **Your Relationship Will Be Better When You Are Married:** Dr. Phil, who was a weekly guest on *Oprah* and now has his own show, suggests that you take a look at your relationship exactly as it is before you get married. If upon examination you feel there is much about it that you don't like, don't fool yourself into thinking that being married is going to change those things—or change him. So wise. Of course, there are things that you can do to improve a relationship—counseling, working on better or increased communication—but marriage is actually not one of those things. It is not a relationship fixer, nor is it intended to be.

2. **You Will Be Financially Better Off:** You might be. I hope you are. But it's also quite possible that you won't be. Look around you. Most women and most moms work whether they want to or not, because most households today require two incomes. And even if you are financially better off when you get married, that doesn't necessarily make life financially carefree. So if you see your wifely responsibilities as cooling out poolside and eating bonbons, think again. Take an

interest in your finances and your financial well-being now because it will still matter down the road.

3. **You and Your Husband Will Share Everything:** It's possible that your future husband will want to spend his free time exactly the way you do. But don't count on it, and don't put your interests on hold in the meantime. The perfect man for you to spend the rest of your life with may very well not share your enthusiasm for scuba diving or antique shopping or football or whatever. And you may not share his passion for jai alai or watercolors or heavy metal. Cultivate relationships with people who do share your interests and pursue those interests with them. You may end up pursuing those interests with those people for the rest of your life, and you and your marriage will be better for it.

4. **Other Things in Your Life Will Be Better:** As if! Marriage does not make your job more interesting or your sister less selfish or your mother more understanding. This may sound obvious to you, but I can't tell you how many people expect to return to a shinier, happier life after their honeymoon. Also, do not expect people in your life who say they want you to get married—or who may even be pressuring you to—to behave better or differently after you do.

5. **You Will Never Be Attracted to Anyone Else Again:** Lucy's father says that we all live in a constant state of desire and that fidelity in marriage is all about making the choice to be faithful. I don't know about a constant state of desire, but very likely you will come across someone besides your spouse in the course of your married life to whom you are attracted. You may not be sure if this snazzy fellow is someone you would have just wanted to shag or whether he could

have been the love of your life in a parallel universe. You'll never know, but it's a touch unsettling, especially if you expected that in addition to actually being faithful, you'd feel you always wanted to be.

Top 5 Albums All Soulful Women Should Own

If you don't already own these albums, I think you should get your hands on every single one of them immediately.

1. **Billie Holiday**—*Stormy Blues*: Billie was not only the absolute best at what she did but she did it so well that it became much bigger than her. Her voice isn't just singing; it's magic *and* it's as familiar as your own heartbeat.

2. **Stevie Wonder**—*Songs in the Key of Life*: Joy. Joy. Joy. And more joy. Sure, he's a musical genius just going about the business of being brilliant, but I don't think I'm the only person who got the feeling from this album that he actually wanted to reach out and make each one of us happier.

3. **Miles Davis**—*Kind of Blue*: This is such a seminal album in music and in jazz that it's almost trite to try to say anything about it. I will say this: It's relatively spare, and it will leave a blue thumbprint on your soul forever.

4. **Aretha Franklin**—*I Never Loved a Man the Way That I Love You*: This is one of Aretha's first albums. It's the album where she created the style and sound that came to define her and came to define the power and passion of a woman for many of us. It has many of her greatest hits on it, like "Respect," "Dr. Feelgood," and "Baby, Baby, Baby," yet it's not a greatest hits album. It's in the exact form that she (and

the producers and record executives) wanted us to hear her back when.

5. **Earth, Wind & Fire**—*Gratitude*: Gratitude is what you feel when you listen to this album—gratitude that it was recorded, gratitude that you have it, and gratitude to be alive and able to listen to it.

QUIZ #5
Is Your Groove Back?

It's a good time to check in and see how much better you are now than you were a mere six months ago. Everyone processes loss at different speeds, but I definitely think that around now you should be feeling at least okay to good.

Is your breakup the first thing you think about in the morning or the last thing you think about at night?
If the answer is NO: Right on.
If the answer is YES: It's normal to think about your ex and your breakup sometimes, but if recovering is still defining your life, you may want to get some additional help. Your life is precious and you don't want to waste time that could be much better spent by dwelling on the past. The best is ahead.

Are you smelling, hearing, seeing, tasting, and feeling the world at least as clearly as you did before the breakup?
If the answer is NO: Continuing dullness of your senses is a pretty good indication that you are not doing very well. As a chunk of time has passed since you and your ex split, you should take charge and explore getting some extra help. You can't fully start enjoying your life until you've recovered your senses (literally), and not enjoying your life is really a crime. Just think of all the trash and smog that awaits your reawakened nose.

If the answer is YES: That is awesome. Now, are you using them to maximize your pleasure?

Have you explored any new or rediscovered interests?
If the answer is NO: What are you waiting for? Are you too busy? Too broke? Come on, there must be something that you can manage now. There is no time like the present to make your life more interesting to you.
If the answer is YES: Mad high fives. It takes a lot of resolve to actually bust out and do something new. You rule.

Are you wearing sexy undies?
If the answer is NO: There is a story about a famous director who, at a rehearsal, notices a young actress schlepping across the stage. He says, "Tomorrow, wear sexy underwear." The actress says, "But, sir, no one will know I'm wearing it." He says, "That's all right. You'll know." And that's my point. Don't save the nice stuff for special occasions—wear it for yourself and often.
If the answer is YES: Excellent.

Do you feel fortunate?
If the answer is NO: Never, or just not right this minute? It's hard to maintain a constant feeling of good fortune, but if you almost never feel lucky, you need to make some changes in your life. Either you have got to create things in your life that make you feel gratitude, or you have got to find a feeling of gratitude for your life as it is.
If the answer is YES: Yeah, baby. Try to always hold onto that

feeling because even if every day isn't sheer bliss, it's good to be alive.

It's either time to break out the bubbly and celebrate the return of your groove, or it's time to put your foot down and do whatever it takes for you to find your groove again. Your life isn't a dress rehearsal. Live it righteously.

Conclusion

If your palms aren't too tired, high-five yourself yet again. You may not be laughing all the time and wildly in love with your life, but there is no doubt that you are feeling a lot better than you did six months ago. Can you even really remember how miserable you felt back then? Most people can summon a vague feeling of horror, but the actual intensity of the pain can't be accessed. That intensity, thank God, does not stand up against the passage of time.

As relieved as you are, you may be wondering why you had

to experience the kind of pain you just endured. I don't have a very good answer for that and neither did my wise grandma. A lot of people try to find meaning in suffering. For example, you may be familiar with the phrase "that which not does not kill us makes us stronger." Maybe it does, but I'm not sure that being stronger makes pain worthwhile. I myself am pain averse—for my friends, for myself, for you. But, of course, most pain that comes our way in life is not a matter of choice. And when it comes, you can live through it or you can throw in the towel— literally or emotionally—and that just isn't an appealing option.

I do think that heartbreak—though again I would never recommend it—has a silver lining. If you can break out of your own pain, the experience can bring a new or renewed sense of compassion into your heart—for others who have experienced what you have and for people the world over suffering in many different ways. Heartbreak can also bring you a new or renewed understanding of the world around you. Listen to Billie Holiday singing "Lover Man," watch *Casablanca*, talk to your widowed great-aunt. Are you hearing or seeing them more clearly?

I remember one time I had my heart thoroughly trounced. I was lying on my bed with the radio on and a blues song came on. I think I'd actually heard it before, but I'd never really listened to it. And it hit me: I understood exactly what was being said. Then I realized that several years earlier when I'd told my grandma about a painful breakup I was going through she had understood exactly what I was saying and then some. While my experience had felt so private and so unique, I realized that I had just joined the world's biggest club. And, in a weird way, I felt proud. I wasn't happy, but I knew I was living and I knew I could be happy again.

Whether you realize it or not, you are probably more soulful, more compassionate, and wiser than you have ever been. And that's just for starters. The future is wide open. There is every reason to believe that you can have the things that you want in this life—including a great relationship. I promise, if nothing else, it will be all the sweeter for your recent experience.

Appendix:

DAYS YOU COULD DO WITHOUT

Your breakup may have happened at a relatively good time in terms of your calendar. But very likely, in the course of your healing, you will have to deal with days that you could do without. I remember, for example, that a boyfriend of mine and I broke up a week before Valentine's Day. On that Valentine's Day, I was doing my best to pretend that it was just another day when a big box came for me. My ex—who was living in Europe at the time—had sent me a Valentine's Day present early to allow for shipping, which was thoughtful but didn't prevent him breaking my heart a day after he sent it. Needless to say, that Valentine's Day blew. Here are some thoughts on how to make it through potentially upsetting days if they come up before you are ready to enjoy them.

Valentine's Day

The horror. I have to say that Valentine's Day is a totally ridiculous holiday. Any holiday where you don't get a paid day off of work is totally wrong to begin with. Furthermore, the number of people who are depressed by the Valentine's Day hooplah is far greater than the number of people who actually enjoy it. That being the case, I can't even understand why Valentine's Day continues to roll around every year.

Anyway, short of starting an anti–Valentine's Day movement and getting into costly litigation with Hallmark, I recommend the following:

- Do not leave home. Call in sick or plan to take the day off. Don't turn on the TV at the risk of being bombarded by obnoxious commercials and do not go on-line because it's like an FTD blitz out there. Rent movies, read, listen to music, light candles, celebrate the fact that you love yourself.
- Get out of town. Change your scenery. Valentine's Day is less obnoxious when you are in unfamiliar terrain. Better still, get out of the country. I don't think Valentine's Day is celebrated in the same lovey-dovey way in the rest of the world as it is here.
- Girl power. This obviously will not work if every one of your girlfriends is in a couple right now. Get a group of the ladies together and invite them over for dinner or force someone else to host everyone. Then crack open some decent wine, throw flowers into the mix, swap Valentine's Day horror stories, and celebrate the fact that you love your friends and that they love you.
- Love power. There is probably someone in your life who not only doesn't have a valentine but doesn't have many friends. Instead of crying yourself a river that you don't have a valentine, why don't you warm someone else's heart with your friendship? Invite him or her over to dinner or bring him or her flowers and dessert. Giving may not always be better than receiving, but it's definitely more noble than wallowing in self-pity.

Your Birthday

Even if you generally enjoy celebrating your birthday, a recent breakup can certainly give you the birthday blues. Here's the thing: Do not do nothing. I guarantee that ignoring your birthday will only make you feel worse. Plus it's miserly to deny the people who love you the chance to shower you with affection and maybe some neat presents. If you can't deal with something elaborate or having to face everyone you know, invite a few people to do something low-key. If you don't feel up to getting dressed, have a pajama party. Unless your birthday is happening only a few days after your breakup, it is actually more depressing to let your ex rob you of your birthright to have a decent time than to have a semi-sad-faced event with a few people you feel really good about. You can always go back to being devastated the next day and you will probably have some extra wine to cry with.

His Birthday

Do not call. Do not send a card. Definitely no gifts and no E-mails. Remember that if his birthday is falling shortly after your breakup, he is probably going to be having a miserable time anyway. But don't feel sorry for him one bit. Use this day to do something that he never wanted to do with you. This is good because it means that you will not run into him and you will spend the day or evening doing something you really like doing that you may not have done often enough when you were together.

Other People's Weddings

I was in a wedding recently and the maid of honor and one of the other bridesmaids were in the first few weeks of breakups. It was not an easy day for either of them, but one of them triumphed over the situation by being gracious, while the other one completely lost it.

Here are some things you want to avoid:
- Getting plastered and making a toast in front of all the guests in which you wish the bride and groom more happiness than you and the ex who dumped you. Then falling off the stage.
- Freaking out on the bride and telling her that the groom is a total loser.
- Making out with more than one person on the dance floor—sloppily.

Here are some tips:
- Do not get too wasted.
- Designate someone—preferably a male friend—to be your escort, dance partner, Kleenex bearer, safety person etc.
- Make yourself useful. Stay busy by volunteering to help with anything.

- If you have to make a toast, write it out in advance and have someone read it over for you before you give it. When you actually make your toast, read it exactly as you wrote it. Save improvising for another day.
- Get on the dance floor and dance. Dance with friends, strangers, that awkward twelve-year-old boy—it'll probably be the biggest thrill of his life so far.

Wedding Showers and Baby Showers

These may have no impact on you whatsoever. Maybe you don't want to get married. Maybe you don't want kids. However, if you do want to get married and/or you want children and you've recently been through a painful breakup, these kinds of events may not be very feel-good right now.

Try to remember that as happy as your friend is at her wedding/baby shower, the change that she is going through is going to bring its fair share of challenges—challenges that you don't have to deal with just yet. She needs your support just as you need her support through your breakup and on lots of other occasions. Also, having a friend break into marriage and childbirth before you will give you better insight when you are getting ready to do the same.

Naturally, it's a good idea to stay relatively sober at these events. And, not surprisingly, it is inappropriate to dominate the conversation with a blow-by-blow account of your breakup.

Anniversaries or Almost

You may find yourself feeling blue on the date that marks the beginning of your and your ex's relationship. Even—and maybe especially—if you did not make it to a year, you may find this day upsetting. Do not wait for the day to creep up on you and bite you in the ass. Make a plan in advance to do something you enjoy on this day. I recommend that you do not spend it alone. If you need some alone time, take it at the beginning of the day. Write in a journal, mope about, cry, whatever. But by the afternoon, get yourself into another space—literally. Put on a groovy outfit and some lipstick and go meet one or several of your friends. It's not a good idea to get too sentimentally attached to an anniversary that in the scheme of the rest of your life is not going to be important. You will have anniversaries with other people and you will probably not even remember the date of this anniversary in a few years. You may be a diva, but it doesn't serve you to be a drama queen.

Holidays

These can be rough, especially if you were planning on spending them with your ex or if you spent them with your ex in the past. It can also be rough if you are spending the holidays with your family and they were expecting you to bring your ex, or bringing your ex was the only way that you were able to conceive of surviving your family's gathering, or you loved spending time with your ex's family. You may also be depressed because holidays seem to be all about family and, with your ex out of the picture, you are feeling a little sensitive about when you will have your own family.

It's good to keep in mind that many many people get depressed and feel lonely around the holidays. You are not the only person for whom they may be a reminder that your life is not exactly where you want it to be. Lots of people don't even have any kind of family or friends to spend the holidays with. Here's how to fight the holiday blues.

- If you are going to spend the holidays with your family, and your family or certain of its members are inclined to make you feel bad because you are not in a couple, do not give them any fodder. You are not a walking pity party. Look your best. Bring something lovely for the holiday meal. Get the people you love the nicest presents that you can afford. And remember that while holidays can bring out the best in families, they can bring out all the craziness too. Brace yourself for it and make "like water off a duck's back" your mantra. You may want to take a few minutes in the bathroom here and there to breathe deeply. Finally, you may want to spend much of the occasion with an "ally" family member who will deflect the potentially annoying comments or behavior of other relatives.
- If your family is cool or some of its members are sensitive individuals, you may want to make it known in advance that you are

a little fragile and that you would appreciate whatever it is that you would appreciate—extra love, no mentions of your ex, etc.

- If you are the one who is going to feel bad being at your family's event alone, fight back by being your best. Plan ahead to do everything you can to make sure that you feel good about yourself when you get there. Maybe you need a haircut or a manicure or a massage. Treat yourself with love and treat yourself like a grown-up. You are one.

- You probably would have spent money on a nice gift for your ex. Take that money and buy a nice gift for yourself. Perhaps something gorgeous to wear that will make you look sharp at the holiday events that you attend. Or take that money and buy something special or useful for someone who really deserves it. Or—and I know this is unlikely—put it in your savings account.

- Do not do nothing. If you were going to spend the holidays with your ex and now you have no plans, make some and fast. Go to your family or get yourself invited to a friend's or have a gathering of people at your house who don't have any plans. One of the best Christmases I ever spent was a disco-Christmas in LA attended by a large group of people who couldn't afford to or didn't want to go home for the holidays. Grandma's house was never so rocking.

- Finally, the holidays are supposed to be about Love. Not about the love between you and one man and 2.5 kids. And you can make a contribution to the bigger picture, wherever you are, by going out of your way to give Love. Maybe you have a housebound relative who would really enjoy a little company. Maybe you have a sick colleague who could use a chicken soup delivery. And almost every town and city has a need for volunteers—even for just a few hours—around the holidays to collect donated food and clothes, to serve meals, to deliver meals, to wrap presents for homeless kids. The list goes on and on. You may not be feeling good, but a little Love from you can make a big difference in the lives of others. And giving will even make you feel better too.

Appendix:

EMERGENCY INFORMATION

Suicide Prevention
National Suicide Prevention Hotline
1-800-SUICIDE
www.cdc.gov/safeusa.htm

Alcohol and Drug Dependence
National Alcohol and Drug Helpline
1-800-821-4357

National Council on Alcoholism and Drug Dependence
1-800-423-4673
www.ncaad.org

Alcoholics Anonymous
1-323-936-4343
www.aa.org

Domestic Violence
National Domestic Violence Hotline
1-800-799-SAFE

National Resource Center on Domestic Violence
1-800-537-2238

Domestic Violence Notepad
www.womenlawyers.com/domestic.htm

Sexual Abuse
RAINN—Rape, Abuse and Incest National Network
1-800-656-HOPE
www.rainn.org

Eating Disorders
American Association of Anorexia and Bulimia
1-212-575-6200
www.aabainc.org

Pregnancy/AIDS/STDs
Planned Parenthood
1-800-230-PLAN
www.plannedparenthood.com

National CDC STD and AIDS Hotline
1-800-227-8922

General Mental Health/Therapy Referrals
National Mental Health Consumer Self-Help Clearinghouse
1-800-553-4539

National Mental Health Association Resource Center
1-800-969-6642

Women's Health
National Women's Health Network
1-202-628-7814
www.womenshealthnetwork.org